Government in the Sunshine State

FLORIDA HISTORY AND CULTURE SERIES

David R. Colburn and
Lance deHaven-Smith

Foreword by Governor Reubin O'D. Askew

Government

# IN THE Sunshine State

## FLORIDA SINCE STATEHOOD

University Press of Florida
Gainesville · Tallahassee · Tampa · Boca Raton
Pensacola · Orlando · Miami · Jacksonville

Copyright 1999 by the Board of Regents of the State of Florida
Printed in the United States of America on acid-free paper
All rights reserved

04  03  02  01  00  99  6  5  4  3  2  1

LIBRARY OF CONGRESS CATALOGING-IN-PUBLICATION DATA
Colburn, David R.
Government in the sunshine state: Florida since statehood / David R. Colburn
and Lance deHaven-Smith: with a foreword by Governor Reubin O'D. Askew.
p. cm. – (Florida history and culture series)
Includes bibliographical references and index.
ISBN 0-8130-1652-5 (cloth)
1. Florida–Politics and government. I. DeHaven-Smith, Lance. II. Title. III. Series.
JK4416.c65  1999  98-36030
306.2'09759–dc21

The University Press of Florida is the scholarly publishing agency for the State
University System of Florida, comprising Florida A&M University, Florida Atlantic
University, Florida International University, Florida State University, University of
Central Florida, University of Florida, University of North Florida, University of
South Florida, and University of West Florida.

University Press of Florida
15 Northwest 15th Street
Gainesville, FL 32611
http://nersp.nerdc.ufl.edu/~upf

The Florida History and Culture Series comprises important works written to promote an understanding of the state's rich history and diversity. Accessible and attractively designed, the books in this series contribute a historical perspective to studies focusing on the environment, politics, literature, material culture, and cultural studies.

EDITED BY RAYMOND ARSENAULT AND GARY R. MORMINO

*Al Burt's Florida: Snowbirds, Sand Castles, and Self-Rising Crackers,* by Al Burt (1997)
*Black Miami in the Twentieth Century,* by Marvin Dunn (1997)
*Gladesmen: Gator Hunters, Moonshiners, and Skiffers,* by Glen Simmons and Laura Ogden (1998)
*"Come to My Sunland": Letters of Julia Daniels Moseley from the Florida Frontier, 1882–1886,* by Julia Winifred Moseley and Betty Powers Crislip (1998)
*The Enduring Seminoles: From Alligator Wrestling to Ecotourism,* by Patsy West (1998)
*Government in the Sunshine State: Florida since Statehood,* by David R. Colburn and Lance deHaven-Smith (1999)

# Contents

Foreword by Reubin O'D. Askew   ix

Preface by Gary R. Mormino and Raymond Arsenault   xi

Acknowledgments   xv

Introduction   1

1. The Evolution of Florida's Government:
   The First Hundred Years   6

2. Florida in the Modern Era   43

3. Florida's Government and Administrative Structure   77

4. Politics, Policy, and Public Opinion   118

5. Reflections on State Government in Florida   146

   Bibliography   151

   Index   155

   Photo sections follow pages 20, 52, 92, 132.

# Foreword

Governor Reubin O'D. Askew

Thomas Jefferson once said that a nation that "expects to be both igno-
rant and free . . . expects something that never was and never will be."
In this nation, we took the concept that people should govern themselves and made it work. The success of the American experiment required the involvement of many good and caring people, and it has
taken the participation of thinking people to ensure its continued success. Jefferson also observed that democracy "begins in conversation."
To ensure the continued success of this great experiment, Americans
have a responsibility to be informed about their government. That responsibility is certainly no less true for Floridians, many of whom are
new to the state and unfamiliar with its history and government.

I strongly encourage all citizens to read this important book so that
they will understand how Florida's history has shaped its current political environment and helped determine the issues that are crucial to the
state's development. The authors have written a book that is fundamental to understanding this state. Readers do not have to be political scientists or professionals to comprehend the evolution of state politics

and the issues that dominate political life at the end of the twentieth century.

As the United States enters a new century as a free and democratic society, we are faced with an unusual opportunity to build upon the heritage of the past to benefit future generations. In the twentieth century, we finally recognized the importance of diversity to the vitality of our democracy and have granted fundamental rights of citizenship to all. We can now move beyond those concerns that have divided us and address issues that will surely enrich opportunities for future generations. It is a great challenge, and we will only succeed if we follow the advice of Thomas Jefferson and recommit ourselves to this great democracy.

Knowledge and democracy will be the keys to the twenty-first century. Other nations and peoples are rapidly embracing the principles of democracy and looking to the United States to guide them. We have a special responsibility in this global community that we have entered: to secure and strengthen our own democracy. If we fail to participate in the electoral process and if we fail to understand our history and current political environment, we risk sacrificing our democracy. This wonderful book by David Colburn and Lance deHaven-Smith provides a starting point for Floridians to recommit themselves to the American experiment. It is essential that we do so.

# Preface

*Government in the Sunshine State* is the sixth volume in a series de-
voted to the study of Florida history and culture. During the past half-
century, the burgeoning population and increased national and international visibility of Florida have sparked popular interest in the state's
past, present, and future. As the favorite destination of countless tourists and as the new home for millions of retirees and other migrants,
modern Florida has become a demographic, political, and cultural
bellwether. But, unfortunately, the quantity and quality of the literature on Florida's distinctive heritage and character has not kept pace
with the Sunshine State's enhanced status.

In an effort to remedy this situation—to provide an accessible and
attractive format for the publication of Florida-related books—the University Press of Florida has established the Florida History and Culture
series. As coeditors of the series, we are committed to the creation of an
eclectic but carefully crafted set of books that will provide the field of
Florida studies with a new focus and that will encourage Florida re-
searchers and writers to consider the broader implications and context
of their work. The series will include standard academic monographs,
works of synthesis, memoirs, and anthologies. We encourage authors

researching Florida's environment, politics, literature, and popular or material culture to submit their manuscripts for inclusion. We want each book to retain a distinct character and voice, but at the same time we hope to foster a sense of community and collaboration among Florida scholars.

As Florida braces for the new millennium, curiosity about the state's past and future appears to be quickening. Throughout modern history, the years marking a century's end have spawned anxiety, reflection, and political action. Two hundred years ago the American and French Revolutions wrought a new order in the world, and a century ago the implications of massive immigration, urbanization, and industrialization sparked a decade of crisis in which American politics and society were radically transformed. Thus, it is not surprising that in late-twentieth-century Florida, where the pace of change has been dizzying, scholars and pundits have begun to ponder the meaning of old revolutions, new retirees, and daily gridlock.

The ambitious goal of David R. Colburn and Lance deHaven-Smith is to come to terms with the forces that have reshaped government and politics in modern Florida. In *Government in the Sunshine State*, they explicate and demystify the complex factors that have contributed to the state's distinctive governmental institutions and traditions. Recognizing that the modern saga of Florida government has been marked by lost opportunities and limited achievements, they offer an unblinking assessment of the state's lingering frontier mentality, political fragmentation, and chronic civic indifference.

As Colburn and deHaven-Smith demonstrate, twentieth-century Florida has experienced a world of change, both quantitative and qualitative. In 1900, the state boasted a mere half-million inhabitants, the majority of whom were native-born Floridians. Comfortable with their Deep South identity, most Floridians lived within fifty miles of the Alabama or Georgia borders. Racial lynchings and antilabor violence occurred with frightening regularity, and vigilantes and public officials routinely intimidated potential African-American voters. The state legislature was busily constructing an all-encompassing codified system of racial segregation, discrimination, and disfranchisement.

Half a century later, Florida still appeared to have at least one foot planted firmly in the nineteenth century. The legislature remained a white male bastion dominated by the rural "Pork Chop Gang"; Jim Crow was still the order of the day; and Florida governors, hamstrung by the restrictions of the outmoded Constitution of 1885, rarely achieved distinction. Nevertheless, as the authors point out, post–World War II Florida was already in the throes of a powerful and profound transformation. World War II and a 1944 Supreme Court decision outlawing white primaries energized local and national civil rights groups, encouraging an increasingly large number of black voters to participate in state and local politics. At the same time, a small but growing cadre of progressive politicians fought for reapportionment, educational improvement, and other reforms. Although the efforts of reformers such as LeRoy Collins were often stymied by the forces of tradition, social and demographic trends buoyed hopes for the future.

At mid-century, Florida was poised for a demographic surge in which the state's population would increase from 2.7 million to nearly 15 million by the late 1990s. This population explosion was a by-product of vast social, economic, and political changes. The growth of the military-industrial complex; the expansion of Social Security and other government programs; the upheavals of the Cold War; the decolonization of the Third World; the growth of tourism; technological innovations such as air-conditioning, interstate highways, and commercial air travel; and the civil rights, environmental, and women's movements have all contributed to the making of modern Florida.

As the respective directors of the Reubin O'D. Askew Institute on Politics and Society at the University of Florida and the Reubin O'D. Askew School of Public Administration and Policy at Florida State University, Colburn and deHaven-Smith are ideally suited to the difficult task of producing a cogent interpretation of twentieth-century government in Florida. Their ability to combine historical and contemporary perspectives and their commitment to lucid, jargon-free prose have made this fast-paced volume a valuable addition to the literature on modern Florida. Readers of this illuminating study will gain not only an understanding of the evolution of Florida government and politics but also a greater appreciation for the daunting public policy challenges that confront today's leaders. Indeed, *Government in the Sunshine State* should be required reading for Florida voters and politicians, especially for those who aspire to lead the state in the twenty-first century.

Raymond Arsenault, University of South Florida
Gary R. Mormino, University of South Florida
*Series Editors*

# Acknowledgments

We owe a great debt of gratitude to a number of colleagues whose work and whose willingness to read all or significant parts of this manuscript helped us immensely. In particular we thank Jeffrey Adler, Michael Gannon, Jamil Jreiset, Lynn Leverty, Gary Mormino, Richard Scher, Robert Huckshorn, and Richard Chackerian, who read the entire manuscript and gave us the benefit of their expertise and critical judgment. We also thank Raymond Arsenault, Manning Dauer, Raymond Mohl, Nancy Hewitt, James Crooks, George Pozzetta, Jane Landers, Steven Lawson, Robert Ingalls, Susan McManus, Samuel Proctor, Joe Richardson, Larry Rivers, Canter Brown, Jerrold Shofner, Bertram Wyatt-Brown, Daniel Schaefer, and Maxine Jones, whose professional scholarship influenced much of our thinking in this book. None of these people is responsible for errors in this book. We accept that responsibility, but we are grateful for their important work on Florida and for their collegial support for this book.

We dedicate this book to our wives, Marion Colburn and Westi Jo deHaven-Smith.

# Introduction

In 1900, Florida's future was uncertain at best. The state had slightly more than a half-million residents (the smallest population in the South), a rural, frontier-like economy, a biracial, segregated society, and an environment that seemed ill suited to substantial development. One hundred years later, Florida is only barely recognizable as the same state. It has a population of nearly 15 million, fourth largest in the United States (see fig. 1), and is one of the most racially and ethnically diverse states in the nation and the most urbanized state in the South. Its economy is dominated by tourism and increasingly influenced by international commerce. Florida is one of the few bellwether states in the nation, with demographics that many believe foreshadow those of most states in the twenty-first century. Politicians and economists are closely watching the developments that are taking place in Florida in order to understand the changes that will affect the rest of the nation.

The transition from a backwater to a bellwether state has been re-markable and traumatic for Florida. It is, nevertheless, what most resi-

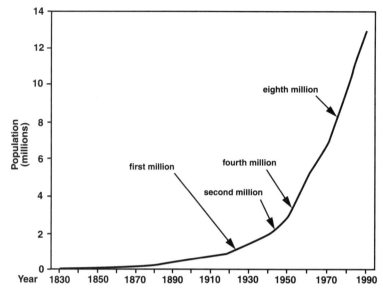

Fig. 1. Population of Florida, 1830–1990.

dents at the turn of the twentieth century sought for their state and for themselves, but what few believed would ever occur in their lifetimes.

Today, in the 1990s, with the benefits of air conditioning and pesticides, people flock to Florida at the phenomenal rate of nearly 645 per day from various places in the United States as well as Canada, the Caribbean, and Central America. For dreamers, Florida represents an economic frontier, a land of renewal and rebirth, much like the land first observed by Juan Ponce de León in 1513. For schemers, it is a place to get rich quick without investing anything of value.

The young who migrate to Florida view it as a place to launch their careers without sacrificing quality of life. For those more seasoned but still searching for their pot of gold, it represents a place to start over. For senior citizens, it offers an environment that allows them to remain vigorous and enjoy their penultimate years.

What intrigues demographers and political scientists about Florida is the way in which the state responds to the needs and concerns of its dynamic and divergent population and how it creates "one" out of the "many" (to quote the state motto) who choose to settle there. Florida has the largest senior citizen population in the United States, with more than 2.5 million people aged over sixty-five (over 18 percent of the population). In fact, Florida's retirement community is larger than the entire populations of some states in the United States. Florida is also increasingly diverse. Migrants from the Caribbean and Central America, who generally settle along the southeast coast, constitute 13.6 percent of the population, with Cuban Americans alone comprising half that number. Florida's African-American population is only slightly smaller, at 13.5 percent.

What also makes Florida fascinating is that the three regions of the state reflect distinct trends that are developing nationally. For example, southeastern Florida has become a vast melting pot of people from throughout the Western Hemisphere, and Miami is a financial metropolis that intersects daily with the Caribbean and South America and that has a significant influence on that region of the world both economically and culturally. On the other hand, Central Florida, with its tourist industries, especially the megacompany Walt Disney World, is often seen as a place for traditional American values, offering the family-oriented lifestyle that many today are seeking. More runaways flee to Orlando than to any other U.S. city, searching for those values that they hope will give their lives meaning. Northern Florida, however, in many ways still resembles the Old South. It is a region of Dixiecrats, lumber companies, farmers, and poor blacks who struggle to secure an existence amidst the challenges of mother nature, middling land, and steadily declining lumber and farm prices.

## Florida's Distinctiveness in the Twentieth Century

Florida remains as unique as when political scientist V. O. Key, Jr., called it "The Different State" in his classic study of southern politics in 1949. The state's heritage extends back to its Native American and Spanish roots, and those influences are still encountered, largely through the names of cities, counties, and rivers. During the nineteenth century, however, Florida abandoned much of its diverse heritage to become part of the Deep South, as settlers from nearby southern states moved across the border. To this day, the state retains a strong southern culture in its northern and Panhandle areas. By the middle decades of the twentieth century, migration into the central and southern parts of the state began to separate Florida from its southern roots and link it to other Sunbelt States like California and Texas. Few other states have had such a diversity of ethnic, racial, and regional influences.

Florida's political traditions make the state as different from its southern counterparts as its diversity does, and this is particularly what caught Key's eye in 1949. The development of a strong two-party system in recent years belies the fact that for much of this century Florida politics was characterized by a single-party system in which there was little personal loyalty. Key characterized it as a system in political chaos, with "every man for himself." Remnants of that system still haunt the Democratic Party in the late twentieth century and have made it vulnerable to the renaissance of the Republican Party.

Florida politics have also been distinctive in other ways. From "government in the sunshine," which makes all government meetings accessible to the public, to the development of one of the first professional staff systems for the state legislature, to a "resign to run" law requiring current officeholders to step down before campaigning for a new position, to the practice of allowing citizen initiatives in amending the Constitution and state law, Florida has helped change the face of state politics in the late twentieth century.

Florida's political environment is also unusual because of the state's extensive urban and regional diversity. Most states have one or two large cities that profoundly influence state politics. Georgia has Atlanta, New York has New York City, California has Los Angeles and San Francisco, Massachusetts has Boston, and Illinois has Chicago. In contrast, Florida is a state of several relatively modest-sized cities—Jacksonville, Miami, Ft. Lauderdale, Daytona Beach, Ft. Myers, Orlando, Tampa, St. Petersburg, Pensacola, Gainesville, Tallahassee, and West Palm Beach— that are scattered throughout its regions. The geographic dispersion of these cities has fostered many political divisions in Florida and some strange political bedfellows during the twentieth century as politicians have sought to build coalitions across urban and regional lines.

These characteristics combine to make Florida politics colorful, complex, confusing, and occasionally bizarre, but seldom dull. Because the state is large and fragmented and ethnically and racially diverse, no single region dominates state politics. Each region produces its own brand of leaders. Unstable coalitions between candidates and parties in the various regions form and reform as issues and concerns shift over time. The whole process is like looking through a kaleidoscope, with each twist of the lens producing a new configuration and a new direction for state politics.

## Understanding Florida Politics

Whether you are new to Florida or one of those rare natives, you probably find the state's politics terribly confusing if not downright mystifying. The character of southern politics in a state that seems so unsouthern has bewildered more than a few newcomers. Moreover, unlike other states, Florida retains the collegial form of executive governance that it created in the late nineteenth century. Referred to as the cabinet system, it requires the governor and six other officials, all of whom are elected statewide, to establish a majority before the executive branch can act. Although other states have executive branches that have some similarities with Florida's in structure, none vests power as extensively as Florida in a system of governance in which a majority of these officials must agree before the executive branch can act.

The relationship between the governor, the legislature, and the State Supreme Court in Florida has much in common with other states, but all three bodies have developed terminology and procedures that often make them accessible only to insiders and not to citizens. Equally mystifying is Florida's system of local government and public finance, with its county, city, and special districts and its multilayered combination of fees, local option taxes, state taxes, bonds, charges on new development, and various other revenue sources.

Florida's local government and financial systems are an outgrowth of its unique history, diverse population, frontier-like society, and agricultural and service economy.

Trying to comprehend the language of Florida politics and the ways in which the past and present have intersected to shape the current political environment is rather daunting for Floridians, especially for those who have only recently moved here. This book is meant to assist them in understanding the political process and the political heritage of the state so that they can make informed decisions as citizens.

# 1
## The Evolution of Florida's Government: The First Hundred Years

### Statehood and Civil War in Florida

"We're a southern state and damn proud of it," a resident of Taylor County in north Florida commented in 1995 as he sat in his pickup truck with a decal of a Confederate flag on the back window, but 300 miles to the south a resident of Dade County looked thoroughly bewildered when he was asked what it meant to be a Southerner. For much of its recent history, Florida has been essentially two states—one that extends south from the Georgia border to Ocala, which has identified with the South and its social, political, and racial traditions, and a second, extending north from Key West and Miami to Orlando, that has a heritage with little connection to the South, a diverse ethnic and racial population, and a conception of the state as part of the national and international economy. On occasion the traditions of one region have influenced those of the other, most notably in the area of racial policy. Nevertheless, to understand Florida's political and constitutional development in the nineteenth and twentieth centuries, one has to be aware of this regional distinctiveness and the difficulties it has created for political leaders as they have attempted to chart a course for the state.

The association of Florida with the Deep South grew out of the migration of people from Alabama, Georgia, and South Carolina to Florida in the nineteenth century. These settlers greatly outnumbered other migrants to the region during the antebellum period, and in the northern regions of Florida from Pensacola to Jacksonville they re-created the southern culture of their former homes. They also brought with them the plantation system and the timber and turpentine industries, reinforcing Florida's social and political ties with its Deep South neighbors.

Although the population of Florida was overwhelmingly concentrated in the northern region, there was a lack of unanimity about the issue of statehood. Many residents of East Florida and West Florida, two sections that had originally been created as separate colonies by Great Britain, favored dividing the territory into two states because each region had geographical and historical ties to the state nearest it. But the mounting national struggle between slave and free states made it unlikely that two slave states would be carved out of Florida. Nevertheless, many residents of Florida were growing tired of territorial status and of having their future determined by representatives of other states. In 1837, by the narrowest of margins (2,065 to 1,961) Floridians voted for statehood. The decisive vote for statehood among residents in Middle Florida (Leon, Jefferson, Gadsden, and Jackson counties) ensured the positive, albeit narrow, majority.

Not surprisingly, the Florida Constitution shared many similarities with those of its neighbors Alabama, Georgia, and South Carolina. Because of the general suspicion of executive leadership, the Constitution restricted the governor to one four-year term and made him ineligible for reelection. Each county was allotted one representative, who served a one-year term but was eligible for reelection. Senators served two-year terms and could also be reelected. They represented districts that were as nearly equal in population as possible. The Constitution revealed a hostility to bankers that extended throughout much of the South and reflected the debtor status of many southern farmers during this era. Bankers were banned from the governorship and the legislature for up to one year after they had ceased employment at a bank. Separation of church and state was also prominently featured, and religious leaders were disqualified from holding state office. Lastly, pro-slavery sentiment pervaded the constitutional convention, and the final document strongly supported the rights of slaveholders and forbade legislative interference in such matters.

The proposed constitution received support from all but one delegate, but it encountered a mixed reception from Floridians in general, as had the vote on statehood, and there was considerable doubt that it would receive the majority of votes necessary for adoption. By the narrow margin of a hundred votes, the Constitution became law in 1839. By no means, however, had Floridians put aside their differences. Supporters of a united Florida and proponents of two Floridas continued to bombard the U.S. Congress on behalf of their separate interests. The historian Charlton Tebeau wrote that these petitions "must have left considerable doubt in that body that Floridians knew what they wanted."

The votes for statehood and for the Constitution provided supporters of one Florida with a momentum that proved difficult for divisionists to overcome. Led by the skillful talents of its territorial delegate, David Levy Yulee, Florida secured support for statehood from the House and Senate in 1845. On March 3, his last day in office, President John Tyler signed the bill making Florida the 27th state. In 1846 Iowa entered the Union as Florida's free-state counterpart.

As the calamitous events of the 1850s moved the nation closer to a bloody division in 1861, Floridians faced inner turmoil, as unionists, former slaves, vigilantes, and those simply opposed to war clashed with secessionists. Governor Madison Starke, an ardent secessionist, quickly sided with the Confederacy, and on January 10, 1861, with widespread support in the legislature, Florida became the third southern state to withdraw from the Union. The commitment of most Floridians to the social and cultural values of the South and to slavery ensured their loyalty to the Confederacy, but inner civil conflict persisted throughout the war years. Despite suffering, turmoil, and eventual defeat during the Civil War, most Floridians never doubted their decision to support the

Confederacy, and in the aftermath of the bloody conflict, they mourned the "Lost Cause" and "worshipped the Confederate dead and hated the Yankee living." Memories of the Civil War and Reconstruction remained burned irrevocably in the minds of Floridians from the end of Reconstruction in 1876 through the first half of the twentieth century.

Florida's leaders, like those in other southern states, did not accept the results of the Civil War willingly. Much of the white anger dealt with the loss of their way of life and the dire economic straits in which they found themselves. At war's end, William Marvin, provisional governor, announced that the state treasury was empty, and Florida owed the federal government $77,520.

At nearly every stage of Reconstruction, Floridians resisted federal controls and took steps to preserve the social, political, and racial traditions of the past. Although the new Constitution of 1865 acknowledged the results of the Civil War by rescinding the ordinance of secession and abolishing slavery, it also instituted a series of "Black Codes" to ensure white dominance and regulate the lives of blacks. Among other features, the codes restricted freedom of movement for blacks and allowed law enforcement officials to hire out arrested blacks if they could not post bond. The system smacked of the reinstitutionalization of slavery. An angry Congress, dominated by representatives from the victorious North, denounced the actions of Florida and the other southern states and on March 3, 1867, passed the Military Reconstruction Acts to oversee the readmission of the seceded states under conditions satisfactory to the northern representatives.

The process of Military Reconstruction traumatized Florida, and its effects would be felt for generations to come. Elements of the Union army, including black soldiers, supervised the process of Reconstruction and the adoption of the Constitution of 1868 for nearly nine years, until 1876. After this painful era, Floridians remained isolated from the national mainstream and mired in rural poverty for much of the late nineteenth and early twentieth centuries. Florida was even an outcast among outcasts within the former Confederacy. In 1880, nine out of every ten Floridians resided in rural areas. Key West was the largest city, with 9,800 residents, and only three cities in the entire state had more than 3,000 inhabitants.

Shortly after the collapse of Military Reconstruction in 1876, native whites reasserted their control of state government and rescinded the 1868 Constitution, which had implemented democratic procedures for voting and seeking political office. No one at the time realized that they would be providing the legal framework for gubernatorial and state politics for the next eighty years. The Constitution of 1885 grew out of the political and racial developments of the Civil War and Reconstruction era, and it represented a backlash against Military Reconstruction and the democratic reforms of the 1868 Constitution. The delegates to the convention deliberately weakened the powers that had been granted to the governor in the 1868 Constitution. The new Constitution prevented the governor from succeeding himself and established a cabinet system to weaken the executive branch. It also abolished the office of lieutenant governor and stripped the governor of the substantial appointment powers that he held under the Reconstruction Constitution. The 1885 Constitution proved quite successful in reducing the authority of the governor and reasserting the dominance of northern Floridians and their culture in state affairs.

As the nineteenth century neared its end, state leaders and citizens anxiously searched for ways to expand the economy, which had failed to recover significantly from the devastating costs of the Civil War and Reconstruction. When the promise of a "New South" appeared at the end of the nineteenth century, with pledges to modernize and industrialize the region and bring it into the national mainstream, Floridians eagerly embraced the movement in hopes it would enable the state to become part of the national mainstream and spur economic development. They actively courted land developer Hamilton Disston, railroad magnate Henry Flagler, and other wealthy investors. But despite their best efforts, and the economic contribution of Flagler in particular, the New South generally stayed well north of Florida, and economic expansion went elsewhere.

At about the same time, Democrats in Florida also reestablished the racial caste system, at first informally and then through laws that permeated the entire state, denying African Americans the rights guaranteed to them by the Constitution. Despite opposition from the state Republican Party and resistance from black residents, who vigorously defended their right to the franchise, the Jim Crow system hardened into law in the 1890s and imposed a subservient status on African Americans until well into the second half of the twentieth century. The ramifications of this racial system, like the Constitution of 1885, profoundly affected state politics throughout this era and well into the twentieth century.

## Political, Economic, and Social Developments from 1890 to 1925

As Florida neared the end of the nineteenth century, its politics remained mired in the past. The racial and cultural traditions of the antebellum era and the events of the Civil War and Reconstruction periods defined the mentality and social outlook of most of its citizens and ensured the loyalty of white Floridians to the Democratic Party. The rise of the Farmer's Alliance or Populist movement in Florida in the late 1880s, with its secret affiliation between white and black farmers, sealed the fate of black Floridians, but not in quite the manner blacks had hoped or envisioned. Seeking to improve their lot during the economic hard times of the 1880s and 1890s, southern and midwestern farmers organized an alliance movement aimed at promoting agricultural concerns in state politics. The organization proposed a series of reforms, radical for the time, that included plans for the establishment of farm cooperatives, state ownership of railroads, and direct election of U.S. senators. White alliance members in the South joined forces with black alliancemen to broaden their base of support, but the whites kept the ties secret for fear that racial concerns would keep southern whites from supporting the movement. When Florida Democratic leaders became aware of the alliance between white and black farmers and its potential for undermining their political control of the state, they instituted a ferocious attack against the movement. Democratic legislators enacted a poll tax to discourage the poor from voting and a multiple-ballot law to confuse those who were not well educated. The purpose of both was to prevent blacks and whites from ever joining forces again at the polls. These same Democrats also passed the Jim Crow laws to prevent whites and blacks from being educated or socializing together, so that racial understanding and cooperation could not continue or develop further.

The Democratic counterattack against Populism was devastating. The poll tax of 1889 was instrumental in taking the vote away from black citizens, but it had a profound impact as well on the ability of rural whites to participate in Florida's electoral process. The $2.00 tax was often more cash than white or black farmers in the state earned in a week (in some cases a month); this was a sum that few could afford. Between 1888 and 1892, the percent of black voters in Florida declined from 62 percent to 11 percent, while the percentage of white voters fell from 86 percent to 59 percent. By the turn of the twentieth century, the Democratic Party had fallen securely into the hands of social and economic elites who strengthened their position when needed simply by paying the poll taxes of those whites and blacks who agreed to support them.

The party, and indeed state politics in general, was heavily influenced by these north Florida elites, most of whom were conservative on issues of race, social matters, and economic reform. But while this group usually dominated state politics, it did not always control it. Religion, class, and race were three factors that, in combination, occasionally rose to challenge its leadership.

By 1901, free from the threat of the Republican Party, black voters, and independent rural, white voters, the "lily-white" Democratic Party thoroughly dominated state politics, but this dominance made it very difficult for the party to confine personal ambitions within the traditional party structure. In 1901, party leaders opted to abandon the nominating convention and party platform as a vehicle for controlling the selection of candidates for office. This change persuaded most politically ambitious Floridians to stay within the Democratic Party by allowing as many candidates as were interested to campaign for state offices through the new primary system. Once Democratic voters had made their choices in the primary, then Democrats would unify behind them in the general election, against the Republican opponents.

This structural change worked well in preventing multiple parties, but it did not prevent the Democratic Party from splintering into a variety of factions. It was not uncommon in this period for as many as five candidates to run for the governorship in the Democratic primary, and the situation worsened in the 1930s and 1940s, when many as fourteen candidates sought the party's nomination at one time. Little unity existed within the party, other than a commitment to the racial caste system and to economic development. V. O. Key, Jr., observed that Florida's political structure was "an incredible melange of amorphous factions," virtually all of which were centered in the Democratic Party. Candidates who were privately sympathetic to the progressive policies of Republican president Theodore Roosevelt (1901–9) or with conservative, probusiness Republicans kept their views to themselves and ran as Democrats if they hoped to capture political office in Florida. The Democratic Party in Florida thus represented a broad mix of political, social, and economic views, which tended to promote personal factionalism and undermine party unity.

During this period, a few central issues dominated state politics. National developments, especially those that occurred within the Democratic Party, occasionally impacted on state politics in significant ways. Race was never far from the forefront of state politics, playing a particularly prominent role from 1890 to 1923 and in the post–World War II era up to 1970. But economic development dominated the concerns of state politicians and Floridians in general. The politicians and the people did not always agree on how that development should occur, and various strategies for economic growth would divide them, but Florida Democrats were committed to developing their state so that rural poverty would not continue to define their future. Such views were readily understandable in a state that was physically larger than any in the southeast but had the smallest population—only 528,000—in 1900.

For most of this period Florida looked as much like a frontier state as a southern state, with a population that was 80 percent rural. Entire areas were literally uninhabited, and many supported only a few families. Floridians were an independent lot, self-reliant and even cantankerous. Outlaws often came to Florida to take advantage of the isolation and independent mindedness of the natives to hide from authorities.

Like other southern states at the beginning of the twentieth century, Florida felt the influence of the Progressive movement, which swept the nation and came to play a prominent role in both the national Democratic and Republican parties. Shaped by a variety of forces, most particularly public reaction to the excesses of the Industrial Revolution, progressives sought to make government more responsive to the needs of the middle class, workers, and voters, especially White Anglo-Saxon Protestants. In Florida, the administrations of Governors William Jennings (1901–5) and Napoleon Bonaparte Broward (1905–9) adopted the rhetoric of the progressives in calling for limitations on the influence of railroad and corporate land interests in the state's development. Both governors were committed to state development, public education for whites, and a state-planned and -directed drainage program for the Everglades. Both also emphasized the needs of everyday Floridians over the railroad owners and land developers. As with other Floridians of their time, they led an erstwhile struggle to find solutions to the state's rural poverty.

During his campaign for governor, for example, Broward repeatedly attacked the efforts of railroad and corporate interests to exploit various sections of the state. The resentment in Florida toward the railroad interests grew out of a belief that much of the prime real estate in Florida was being usurped by the railroads and developers. Farmers were also convinced that railroads discriminated against them by charging high rates for shipping their goods to market to offset the reduced rates they granted to large citrus and industrial interests. Many native Floridians saw railroad owners as interlopers, or, even worse, as northerners who sought to enrich themselves at the expense of the state and its citizens.

The development of the state and the debate about who would decide its course constituted one of the two dominant issues in the first decade of the twentieth century. Governors Jennings and Broward carried the fight on behalf of the citizens of the state, but their efforts were hampered by the state's inability to pay for the costs of development, whether the Everglades or any other area. Florida was simply too poor to be able to convince investors that it could guarantee the bonds for such projects. The state never imposed an extractive tax on its natural resources, allowing others to exploit them for their own profit. Florida may well have been able to provide for its citizens if it had had the political will to adopt such a tax. But that will was missing. Jennings and Broward encountered strong opposition within the legislature to their proposals to have the state assume a greater role in development because of the financial costs and also from probusiness elements in Florida, who saw no conflict of interest between the needs of business and of the public.

For the first decade of the century, progressives like Jennings, Broward, and Broward's successor Albert Gilchrist (1909–13) controlled the governor's office, but because of their limited power and sharp divisions within the legislature, they gradually yielded to more entrenched, conservative forces in the state. Progressivism was never as strong in Florida as it was elsewhere, although the city manager form of government did begin in Daytona Beach and spread to other communities in the state and nation. Nevertheless, the Progressive movement never had the impact in Florida that it had in states like Wisconsin, New York, and Ohio, where governors and legislatures enacted reforms to protect citizens and consumers from the worst abuses of industrialism.

Progressivism in Florida suffered because the state lacked the economic resources to transform progressive policies into law and because growth and development remained the highest priorities. The state's progressives also faced strong opposition from forces that were allied with or sympathetic to railroad magnates, land developers, lumber interests, and phosphate mine owners. Even Florida progressives could not avoid the influence of men like Henry Flagler, former partner with John D. Rockefeller in the Standard Oil Corporation and the builder of the Florida East Coast Railroad from Jacksonville to Key West. The chummy relationship between political leaders and businessmen was never more obvious than when Governor Jennings signed a special divorce bill in 1901 so that Flagler could divorce his wife, who was in a mental institution, and remarry. Succumbing to Flagler's economic influence was such a public embarrassment that legislators quickly rescinded the law, but Flagler had what he wanted as others had before him.

The opponents of progressivism, and even some of its allies, believed that cheap land and private development, even in areas as environmentally sensitive as the Everglades, were essential to the state's emergence from poverty. At this stage in Florida's development, environmental concerns took a very distant second place to concerns about economic growth and population expansion. Florida's flirtation with progressivism was thus a short lived affair, and by 1912 political power had fallen into the hands of spokesmen for developers and corporate interests. The coming of World War I sealed the fate of progressivism in Florida, as it did in the rest of the nation, focusing attention on events overseas and on domestic affairs related to the war.

Race constituted the second major characteristic of this era in Florida. As with their counterparts in other southern states, white Floridians saw no contradiction in their efforts to strengthen democracy and to deny equal rights to African Americans. The progressive movement in Florida was a white man's movement, and it sought to protect the rights of white citizens against the power of railroads and land developers and also against the black man. White Floridians carried two banners, one for progressive reform and the other for white supremacy, without a second thought. During his message to the legislature in 1907, for example, Napoleon Broward proposed that the U.S. Congress purchase territory, either foreign or domestic, and transport blacks there so they could live separate lives and govern themselves. "I believe this to be the only hope of a solution of the race problem between the white and black races," Broward wrote. Black Floridians resisted efforts to deport or segregate them, but, with limited resources and few allies, they gradually succumbed to white insistence on legal segregation. Historian Howard Rabinowitz has argued that, given the limited choice between exclusion, advocated by Governor Broward and others, and segregation, blacks preferred segregation. Florida adopted most of its statewide segregation ordinances in the early twentieth century, and the local laws were firmly in place by 1910.

The election of southern-born Woodrow Wilson as president in 1912 and the onset of World War I had a twofold impact on Florida and on the South more generally. With Wilson's election, the South felt that it had been redeemed, and its sense of regional alienation began to diminish. Also, its involvement in the war effort and the social dislocation that resulted from mobilization caused considerable consternation in the South about race relations. Having imposed segregation in the previous decade, white southerners were in no mood in 1917 to alter the system. By contrast, black southerners viewed the war as an opportunity to cast off the oppressive blanket of segregation and lay claim to racial equality by demonstrating their patriotism.

Whites in Florida had mixed feelings about black participation in the war effort. Grove owners, lumber and turpentine interests, and those businessmen generally dependent on a large supply of cheap, black labor did not want their workers going off to war. But others worried that, if only whites were conscripted, black men would greatly outnumber the remaining white men and thus constitute a major threat to the security of white women.

Not surprisingly, given this context, the war years had a tumultuous effect on Florida's race relations. Whites resorted to legal and extralegal violence during the war years and the immediate postwar period to maintain prewar racial patterns. The revival of the Ku Klux Klan in 1915 and its embrace by community leaders reflected the racial concerns of most whites. Black soldiers, who experienced the liberating effects of living and training in northern communities and in Europe, where they found they could move about much more freely than in the South, looked forward to the postwar period and the freedom and opportunity they felt they had earned.

Racial patterns in Florida and the South were further complicated by the massive migration of African Americans to the Midwest and Northeast, which began around 1900 and increased throughout the next decade, peaking in 1915 and again in 1919 and 1920 following the war. Seeking to escape the oppression of segregation and the economic havoc created by the boll weevil's devastation of the cotton crop, blacks were also drawn north by the promise of economic opportunity and greater freedom. From 1910 to 1920 over 40,000 black Floridians joined 283,000 African Americans from other southern states in the migration to Chicago and other midwestern and northeastern cities, where a shortage of immigrant labor as a result of the war had created a great demand for workers. Labor agents from northern industries and railroads descended on the South in search of black workers. The Pennsylvania Railroad, for example, recruited 12,000 blacks to work in its yards and on its tracks, all but 2,000 of whom came from Florida and Georgia.

The response of Florida's whites to the massive departure of black residents was mixed. Initially, whites either ignored or expressed satisfaction with the exodus. As the massive outmigration, especially from the northern counties of Florida, continued during the war years, Governor Park Trammell (1913–17) and his successor, Sidney J. Catts (1917–21), essentially ignored it and black complaints about racial conditions in Florida.

They also ignored complaints from the remaining blacks about racial conditions in Florida. Trammell, no friend of black Floridians, had disregarded the lynching of twenty-nine blacks when he was the state's attorney general and twenty-one lynchings during his governorship. Catts, a political and religious maverick who threatened traditional Democratic rule in Florida, offered no new opportunities for the state's black citizens. Once in office, he publicly labeled black residents as part of "an inferior race," and he refused to criticize two lynchings in 1919. When the NAACP complained about the lynchings, Catts denounced the organization, declaring, "Your Race is always harping on the disgrace it brings to the state by a concourse of white people taking revenge for the dishonoring of a white woman, when if you would . . . [teach] your people not to kill our white officers and disgrace our white women, you would keep down a thousand times greater disgrace."

Catts changed his tune when citrus owners and business leaders, especially in the lumber and turpentine industries, began to complain that the continued outmigration of blacks was having a devastating effect on labor availability and labor costs in Florida. Shifting positions, Catts urged blacks to stay in Florida, calling for unity and harmony among the races. Few black citizens trusted him, however. The migration continued to escalate as a quiet protest against racial conditions in the state and the South in general.

During the early 1920s, white Florida violently suppressed the aspirations of its remaining black population, and state governors played a willing hand in this process. They ignored or refused to protect black citizens, defending their actions by asserting the inferiority and dependence of the black race and receiving ample encouragement from scholars at the nation's leading universities and popular authors, who claimed that scientific evidence documented black inferiority. Black citizens, however, resisted segregation by whatever means were at their disposal. In Ocoee, Florida, in November 1920, for example, blacks attempted to go to the polls and vote, only to be physically assaulted and see their homes and community virtually destroyed.

During this period, the white commitment to maintaining white supremacy knew few bounds. In both Perry and Rosewood, blacks were killed and their property destroyed following alleged assaults by blacks on white women. When blacks in Rosewood tried to defend themselves against a white mob during the first week of January 1923, their public buildings, churches, and homes were burned to the ground; eight people were reported murdered; and black residents were chased from the community, never to return. The promise of freedom that the war seemed to offer never materialized in Florida. By 1924, in the aftermath of Rosewood, black hopes for equality had been completely snuffed out, with state leaders serving as willing accessories in the process.

The reactionary politics of this era also impeded the efforts of women to obtain the vote. Florida refused to support the submission of the nineteenth amendment to the Constitution to voters, and Floridians did not officially ratify the suffrage amendment until 1969, when it did so symbolically, on the fiftieth anniversary of the founding of the Florida (State) League of Women Voters. Much like in other southern states, white men in Florida placed white women on a pedestal as exemplars of white superiority and genteel behavior. They did not wish to see women sullied by such a common and manly pursuit as politics. The gendered construction of Florida society confined women as tightly as the corsets they wore. Nevertheless, as soon as the nineteenth amendment was adopted in 1921, women in Florida went to the polls to vote, and two—Mrs. Katherine Tippetts of St. Petersburg and Mrs. Myrtice Vera McCaskill of Taylor County—ran for state office. Although both were defeated, it quickly became clear that women in Florida would not sit passively by and let men decide the political direction of the state. In 1928, Mrs. Edna Giles Fuller of Orange County became the first woman elected to state office in Florida as a member of the House of Representatives.

The leading voices for women's issues during this period were May Mann Jennings, wife of former governor William S. Jennings, and the Florida State League of Women Voters. Jennings and the league championed such reforms as the right of women to serve on juries and the right of women to manage their own property. They also launched reforms in the environmental and safety arenas. Despite their efforts, however, the southern and racial culture of the state made it exceedingly unlikely that women in politics would be taken seriously prior to 1945.

Even though he was governor of Florida during this reactionary period and was a supporter of segregation and political restrictions on women, Sidney Catts nevertheless represented more than just another conservative Florida politician. Catts had stepped down from the pulpit to seek the governorship in 1916 on a platform that denounced the Catholic Church, corporations, and alcoholism. During the Democratic primary, he lost narrowly to state treasurer William V. Knott, amidst widespread allegations of voter fraud. The *Ocala Weekly Banner* reflected the confusion of most Floridians, pledging to vote for "the Democratic nominee whoever it is." When the State Supreme Court upheld Knott's victory, Catts accepted the Prohibition Party's nomination, armed himself with two pistols to protect himself against what he alleged were Catholic threats on his life, and drove from town to town in a truck equipped with a calliope to signal his arrival. He broke the cycle of Democratic governors who had risen through the party ranks or enjoyed family connections with prominent Democratic leaders and became the only third-party candidate to be elected governor in Florida in the twentieth century. During his governorship, Catts played upon white concerns about ethnic, racial, and religious differences and about corporate power to mobilize a large political following. With support from many Floridians of modest means, he took steps to protect the interests of white farmers and workers and to improve public education. His challenge to traditional Democratic leadership in the state was unwelcome, and party leaders looked for various measures to prevent the rise of his ilk again, including passage of the Sturkie resolution blocking any person from voting in the Democratic primary who opposed a candidate because of his religious views. How they proposed to decide this was never determined. The measure only increased the popularity of Catts and his supporters—known as kittens.

Andrew Jackson, president of the United States from 1829 to 1837, served as the first territorial governor of Florida in 1821. He was glad to return to his native Tennessee and be rid of Florida and its bugs and pests. (State Photographic Archives)

The automobile had begun to make itself felt in Florida by 1904 and would shape the state for the rest of the twentieth century. This photograph, taken at Seabreeze Beach in Daytona, showed cars and bathers vying with one another for space on the beach. (Florida State Archives)

Governor William Sherman Jennings and his father-in-law, Senator A. S. Mann, in a so-called Florida Automobile at St. Augustine about 1903. Jennings led the progressive movement in Florida and his wife, May Mann Jennings, became a champion of women's rights and state environmental needs. (Florida State Archives)

Governor Napoleon Bonaparte Broward took the oath of office on the steps of the old capitol in Tallahassee on January 5, 1905. Retiring governor William Sherman Jennings was standing directly in front of the column at the right. Broward became a dynamic governor whose support of the common man and the economic needs of the state won him a loyal political following. (Florida State Archives)

Governor Albert Gilchrist (*seated at the center*), shown meeting with the staff of the Florida National Guard, made active use of the guard to assist business leaders in breaking labor strikes in Florida. (Florida State Archives)

Rail passengers ride on a steam engine on the Jacksonville, St. Augustine & Halifax Railway Company. From twenty-four short rail lines such as this one, Henry M. Flagler built the Florida East Coast Railway Company that by 1916 extended from Jacksonville to Key West and had 522 miles of track. Flagler's company helped make many parts of Florida accessible to development and commercial activity. (Florida State Archives)

Governor Sidney J. Catts in his inaugural parade in January 1917. He was elected as the candidate of the Prohibition Party, the only person to be elected governor in the twentieth century under the banner of a third party. An electrifying personality, he drove his Ford throughout much of the state to take his candidacy to the people. (Florida State Archives)

Governor Sidney Catts (*seated, left front*) with his family on the steps of the governor's mansion. Catts appointed several members of his family to state positions, for which he was roundly criticized by his political opponents. Loyalty to Catts underscored nearly all his appointments and led the press to refer to his administration as "Catts and his kittens." (Florida State Archives)

Governor Cary Hardee delivering his inaugural address on January 4, 1921. An elegant figure with pince-nez and cutaway tuxedo, he fit the more traditional image of governor after four tumultuous years under Sidney Catts. Hardee was fortunate in that his administration basked in Florida's economic boom. (Florida State Archives)

Before modern highway motels were built, tourist camps like the one pictured here sprang up all over Florida. This "Tin Can Tourist Camp" near Gainesville dated from the post–World War I era when Americans began to flock to Florida. Tourism began to reach the masses and eventually became the engine that drove Florida's economy. (Florida State Archives)

The hurricane of September 18, 1926, signaled the end of Florida's economic boom of the 1920s. It hit southeast Florida without warning, destroying 5,000 homes and damaging 9,000 more from Miami to Ft. Lauderdale. As locals remembered it, "It blowed a crooked road straight and scattered the days of the week so bad Sunday didn't get around 'til late Tuesday morning." (Florida State Archive)

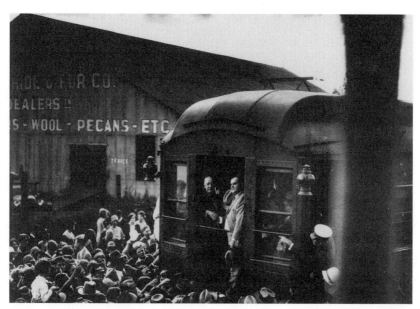

Governor John Martin welcoming Democratic presidential candidate Al Smith of New York in 1928. Despite a general antipathy toward the Republican Party in the state, Florida voters could not bring themselves to vote for Smith, an Irish Catholic and member of Tammany Hall, New York's political machine. Neither did his New York accent help him woo Floridians and other southern voters. (Florida State Archives)

Governor John Martin met with the state's most prominent tourist and the nation's leading industrialist, John D. Rockefeller, at Ormond Beach in 1925. The two men discussed the state's tourist and land boom, which unfortunately collapsed a year later. (Florida State Archives)

Governor David Sholtz (*center*) rode with President Franklin D. Roosevelt and Mayor John T. Alsop of Jacksonville during the president's visit to Jacksonville. Sholtz supported Roosevelt and was happy to receive New Deal funds during some of the bleakest days of the depression. (Florida State Archives)

## Boom and Bust, 1920–1940

Although Catts and his kittens remained political factors throughout the 1920s, the governorship returned to the hands of Democratic Party stalwarts in 1920, with the election of Cary Hardee (1921–25), who took office just in time to bask in the prosperity of an economic boom in south Florida. The economic development and population expansion that Florida had long sought had begun to occur, and Florida's citizens gradually turned their backs on Catts's emphasis on class, religion, and racial difference as the state's economic growth gave them hope for the future. To encourage further development, the state legislature adopted a homestead exemption, excluding the first $25,000 in value from local property taxes, as an added inducement to its constitutional prohibition against an income tax. Growth was so dramatic that Florida's political leaders did little else than hop aboard the roller coaster. Towns sprang up along the coast and in what were formerly swamps. Floridians and people from around the country rushed to become part of the "gold coast" development in the southeast. From 1920 to 1930, the state's population increased by a half million, from 968,470 to 1,468,211. Miami quadrupled in size, from 29,571 to 110,637, becoming the state's second largest city behind Jacksonville, which had 129,549 residents. Tampa and St. Petersburg also boomed, and by 1930 their combined population stood at 141,586. Property on Miami Beach, which Carl Fisher offered to give away in 1915, went for $25,000 or more an acre in the early 1920s. Cities and counties threw caution to the wind as each tried to wrest the golden goose from West Palm Beach and Miami. Most ended up in debt or bankrupt from constructing road and tourist facilities in the belief that if you build them they will come. They did not. As with all roller coasters, Florida's economy suddenly lurched downward in 1925, and Floridians were ill equipped and ill prepared to do anything about it. Buoyed by the new wealth, state leaders had done little to regulate speculators or to restrain the massive debt that towns and counties incurred in an effort to attract investors. By 1926, three years before the rest of the nation, Florida was in a depression, and it remained mired in economic crisis for fourteen long years.

Florida became a metaphor for the boom-and-bust era of the 1920s, and no state experienced the highs and lows any more thoroughly than Florida. Signs of decline appeared in 1925, when newspapers and magazines warned investors about land fraud in Florida. In 1926 a severe hurricane suddenly revealed Florida's environmental vulnerability, completely swamping Miami Beach and causing 392 deaths in the state. When it was followed in 1928 by an even more severe storm, which left an estimated 2,000 Floridians dead, investors withdrew en masse. A fruit fly infestation that devastated 72 percent of the state's citrus trees and the onset of the national depression in 1929 added the final coup de grace. Per capita spending in Florida declined by 58 percent in the five years from 1926 to 1931. State and local tax collections fell from $62.23 to $47.84 per capita, and state banking reserves virtually collapsed from $593 million to a mere $60 million. Nearly 220 banks in the state failed. By the time the stock market collapsed in the fall of 1929, Florida had already been mired in three years of depression so severe that counties had to forfeit on their bonds, close their schools, and in some cases declare bankruptcy.

The financial collapse paralyzed political leaders. Governor Doyle Carlton (1929–33) attempted to counter the prevailing political ineptitude by urging the legislature to raise taxes to reduce a state deficit of $2.5 million and to assist counties in paying off their bonds. He also sought a gasoline tax to pay for roads and to keep schools open. But the governor's tax plan encountered stiff opposition from those representatives whose counties, most of which were in north Florida, had small debts and felt they were being forced to pay for the sins of those who had risked all during the boom years. Fistfights broke out during legislative debates while the economy continued to worsen. At one point a totally exasperated Carlton pleaded with legislators: "If the program that has been offered does not meet with your liking, then for God's sake provide one that does."

Carlton's successors, David Sholtz (1933–37) and Fred Cone (1937–41), refused to follow Carlton's controversial lead and instead urged economy in government. Eight candidates sought the governorship in 1932, and fourteen more tried in 1936, leading political pundits to suggest that a man had to run for governor in order to make a living in

Florida during the depression. Both Sholtz and Cone blamed Florida's problems on irresponsible leadership and called for a return to fiscal restraint, balanced budgets, and sound business principles. Decimated by the state and national depression, Florida looked to the federal government more than most states for assistance. With nearly 30 percent of the population unemployed and state governors offering little hope or vision, voters embraced the 1932 Democratic candidate for president, Franklin D. Roosevelt, with a sense of desperation, hoping that his election would provide Florida with much needed federal assistance.

Roosevelt and the New Deal provided the lifeline that kept Florida afloat during the 1930s. In particular, the Agricultural Adjustment Act provided crucial assistance for financially desperate farmers and grove owners. Also, Roosevelt's buoyant attitude and his ties to the South arising from his winter home in Warm Springs, Georgia, gave encouragement and hope for the future. Governor David Sholtz cast the fate of his administration with the New Deal and his personal relationship with Roosevelt. This secured for Florida a safety net that halted the downward spiral in state and personal finances. Rumors circulated that Sholtz had also secured his own safety net by secretly receiving funds from Florida's pari-mutuel interests. Despite Roosevelt's leadership and aid from the federal government, however, Florida continued to suffer greatly during the depression, and, while the economy began to stabilize in 1936, no real signs of prosperity were in sight as late as 1939.

By the beginning of World War II, Florida had seen its population expand to 1.9 million, but much of the state remained sparsely settled. Orlando, for example, was a town of fewer than 40,000 people, and much of the southwest coast of Florida was relatively undeveloped. Ft. Myers had a population of only 10,600. Despite the brief boom in the 1920s, Florida had changed remarkably little since 1900. The Democratic Party still had a hammerlock on state politics, and representatives from north Florida controlled both houses of the legislature. Republicans had no representation in the legislature at all until Alex Akerman of Orlando was elected in 1945. Black Floridians continued to suffer under the oppression of segregation, and the depression had taken a devastating toll on black family life. Young black men followed the railroads north in a desperate search for opportunity. Only the relatively meager assistance that flowed from New Deal agencies and passed through the hands of white farmers and citrus owners found its way into the pockets of black farmers and prevented them from becoming completely destitute. The state still depended on agriculture and lumber for most of its economic vitality, much the same as it had in the first decade of the twentieth century. Florida's political and economic leaders sought growth under nearly any condition, especially after more than a decade of depression. With the growth of Miami and Tampa, the state's population gradually shifted, so that by the 1930s most Floridians lived in cities.

Despite this population shift, however, Floridians still viewed themselves as a small-town folk, and they continued to hold tightly to conservative political, religious, and social values. The depression had curtailed their optimism about the future and their confidence in the state's political leadership. But this was about to change. World War II finally ended Florida's long economic depression and launched an era of dramatic growth that would transform the state forever.

## Florida Politics at Mid-Century

In examining southern politics on the eve of World War II, V. O. Key observed that Florida was different from other southern states and that the state Democratic Party suffered from extreme political infighting. He attributed Florida's unique political development to its extended geography and the large influx of newcomers from the North, factors that undermined the unity of the Democratic Party. Key reasoned that because of these conditions and because Florida had a relatively small black population (constituting a majority in only three small counties), the state would be the first in the South to develop a viable two-party system. Without the threat of a black majority, Key wrote, the ability of state Democrats to use the race card to unify white voters would diminish in time and allow for the reemergence of the Republicans.

Little did Key realize that Florida's Democratic Party would dominate postwar state politics every bit as thoroughly and for nearly as long as it did in those southern states with large black populations. For approximately ninety years, from the post-Reconstruction period all the way to the late 1960s, all statewide elections were effectively decided within the Democratic Party. The general election, during which Democrats seldom bothered to campaign, only confirmed the decisions made by voters in the party primary.

Had Key misjudged Florida? In one sense, his hypothesis was correct. The race card never had the same impact in many areas of Florida as it had in such states as Mississippi, Georgia, Alabama, and South Carolina, where the size of the black population, and therefore its perceived threat to white domination, served as a constant source of political concern and a rallying force for white voters. But race did play an important factor in areas north of Ocala, where the black population was quite large. For northern Floridians race did indeed matter, and they controlled the state Democratic Party during this era, and therefore state politics. While south Floridians did not embrace the racial values of the north, they showed little interest in lobbying for racial change or the diminution of white supremacy.

What Key also failed to appreciate fully was the political fragmentation created by massive population growth in Florida, which began in the 1920s and accelerated dramatically during and after World War II. In the immediate post-Reconstruction era, most Floridians lived within fifty miles of the Georgia border, and this region of the state was able to capitalize on its majority to dominate the state legislature, control the Democratic Party, and establish an apportionment system that ensured this region's legislative supremacy until the late 1960s, despite a provision in the 1885 Constitution that called for reapportionment every ten years. Ironically, north Florida's dominance was aided by the massive inflow of newcomers during the second half of the twentieth century. With an average of nearly 1.8 million people arriving in each decade from 1940 to 1990, and with most of them settling in south Florida, the region south of Ocala came to have a majority of the state's inhabitants by the 1950s. The concerns of the newcomers focused chiefly on local matters, however, and not on securing and holding statewide political control. Moreover, these new residents were by no means unified. For example, many who came from the northeastern United States had been lifelong Democrats, and they felt reasonably comfortable, at least initially, within Florida's Democratic Party.

U.S. Senator Bob Graham, a native of Miami, attributed the failure of these migrants to change Florida politics to what he called the "Cincinnati factor." In Graham's view, folks from Cincinnati moved to Florida, but for all practical purposes they remained Cincinnatians. They returned to Cincinnati at least once a year to visit family and friends; often sent their children to colleges in Ohio; subscribed to Cincinnati newspapers; voted only to oppose new taxes, which they had resented when they lived in Cincinnati; and, at the end of their lives, had their remains shipped to Cincinnati for burial. They were Floridians only by residence.

The consequence of the Cincinnati factor was that the culturally and economically homogeneous region of north Florida was able to maintain control of the state Democratic Party and through it dominance of state politics. Key saw this population fragmentation taking place even in the 1930s, but he underestimated its long-term consequences for the Democratic Party and for Florida politics.

Thus, despite the dramatic transformation that had occurred in Florida in the post-1920 period, state politics remained unchanged. On the surface, the state appeared little different from its southern neighbors, but below that surface, it was experiencing dynamic changes, and the effects of these changes would inevitably make themselves felt as the state entered World War II.

### World War II and Political and Social Change

Although Florida's economic development was probably inevitable given its semitropical climate, its lengthy and languorous coastline, and its lush environment, the state's revitalization did not commence until the 1940s, with the onset of massive federal expenditures in Florida and the migration of 2,122,100 men and women into the state for military training. The federal government opened military bases throughout Florida to meet the demands of the Navy and Air Force in particular, and tens of thousands of laborers poured into the state to work at air bases and in shipyards in Jacksonville, Panama City, Pensacola, and Tampa. Miami Beach alone saw 70,000 hotel rooms taken over by the

Army Air Force in 1942. The arrival of service personnel, workers, and their families led to the dramatic expansion of its cities from Miami to Jacksonville and west to Pensacola and quickly generated full employment in the state. The federal government further fueled development, funding the construction of modern transportation facilities to connect the cities.

The introduction of effective mosquito control during this period made the state even more appealing to new arrivals and helped awaken many to the state's enormous economic potential. To all but the hardiest of souls, Florida's five-month summer was almost intolerable, but pest control suddenly made the early summer, at least, bearable. The gradual introduction of air conditioning in the 1950s made the entire summer enjoyable. The rest of the year had always been appealing to the rich; with new roads it now became accessible to the middle class.

Led by Governor Spessard Holland (1941–45), Florida worked closely with the Roosevelt administration and the War Department to secure federal funds for Florida. Holland's successor, Millard Caldwell (1945–49), dramatically expanded the activities of the Florida Department of Commerce, attracting new business and visitors into the state to offset the possibility of a postwar economic decline. Commerce Department employees took a devilish pleasure in sending photographs of beautiful scantily clad bathing beauties lounging around a pool or at the ocean to northern newspapers in the dead of winter. Whether it was the ads or better roads and better automobiles, "snowbirds" from as far north as Canada came in search of warm weather and the fountain of youth. Many found both, and Florida's economy experienced no postwar recession.

The state's sales pitch to prospective businesses and residents remained essentially the same throughout the period from 1945 to 1980. Emphasizing low taxes, a healthy environment, cheap land, and a pro-business political climate, state agencies, led by the governor's office, appealed to potential residents and investors throughout the nation, but especially to those east of the Mississippi. The war boom, a healthy postwar national economy, tourism, good roads, and later air conditioning were all instrumental in making the appeal successful. Governor Caldwell undertook a series of trips to the North and Midwest to recruit new business and commerce. These trips expanded in subsequent administrations to include Western Europe, Latin America, and the Far East, as Florida sought to internationalize its economy and promote tourism. The state continued to modernize its roads to accommodate increasing automobile traffic and economic development. As tourism expanded, Caldwell's successor, Fuller Warren (1949–53), pushed through a fence law to keep the cattle from crossing the roads, causing automobile accidents, and killing residents and tourists. By accepting the fence law, Florida crossed the Rubicon and acknowledged that the health and well-being of tourists meant more to the state's future than agriculture.

During the 1940s, nearly 900,000 people moved to Florida, despite the dislocation and lack of permanence produced by the war. Florida had been discovered once again, but, unlike the decade of the 1920s, this time the discovery would have permanent implications.

The war also created new opportunities for the half-million black residents of Florida, and war propaganda gave many hope that racial change would soon be forthcoming. The protracted length of the war, in contrast to the eighteen months of U.S. participation in World War I, along with the social and geographic dislocation caused by it, mobilized the black community behind the goal of racial reform in ways the country had not seen previously. National NAACP leaders called for a "Double V" campaign: victory against racism overseas and racism at home. The campaign to defeat Germany and Japan placed the United States and its state governments in a very awkward position, with officials trying to mobilize the public behind the war effort while simultaneously attempting to maintain segregation in the South. Not surprisingly, federal officials found it increasingly difficult to defend southern racial policies while condemning German racism. Despite the general resistance to racial change throughout the United States, black Americans were discovering more and more allies on the federal bench and in the federal government.

The potential social and political upheaval threatened by Florida's dramatic population growth and the demands of its black citizens did not escape the attention of legislative leaders from north Florida. Efforts to reapportion the legislature in response to the growth of south Florida suddenly became much more politically significant. Few such proposals ever made it to the floor of either chamber in the 1940s and 1950s, however.

Determined to protect their political hegemony as well as the interests and values of their region against those of the new residents of south Florida, north Florida representatives beat back all efforts to lessen their power. Efforts by Governor Millard Caldwell and his successors to reorganize and streamline state government met with consistent legislative opposition. Even under a governor like Caldwell, who shared the political and social convictions of north Floridians, rural legislators were reluctant to strengthen the governor's office at their expense. These same legislators also understood that, because of the growth of south Florida, the ability of north Florida to control the governor's office in the future was limited at best.

With the expansion in the number of executive agencies during the war and the postwar period, Caldwell expressed repeated frustration over his inability to govern the state effectively as it tried to accommodate its massive population influx. Caldwell ruefully noted that, prior to entering office, he spent days appointing thousands of officials to various boards and commissions, including professional licensing boards and local memorial commissions, instead of focusing his energies on the needs and concerns of the state.

While Florida and its political leaders basked in the postwar economic boom, they kept a wary eye on racial developments and sought to do what they could to maintain continuity in race relations. In Florida, Governor Caldwell and his successors Fuller Warren and Dan McCarty complied with the federal courts, but they stonewalled implementation of the decisions at every turn. Caldwell, for example, persuaded the legislature to adopt a Minimum Foundations Program for the public schools. This type of legislation was common in the postwar South and had two essential purposes. The first was to strengthen the educational system in the region through increased funding so that southern states would be more competitive in recruiting and developing new businesses and could create more economic opportunity than had traditionally been available. The second aim, however, was to upgrade black schools so that the federal courts could not charge that public education in Florida was unequal. This effort required a substantial investment from the southern states because black schools had fallen into acute disrepair from lack of funding. But southern states, including Florida, were willing to pay to upgrade them to avoid public school desegregation.

To make sure that segregation barriers remained intact, local leaders and law enforcement officials, often in cooperation with white militants, also took action. Throughout Florida, county sheriffs assisted grove owners, lumbermen, and farmers to see that black veterans shed their uniforms and returned to work in the groves and fields. Deputies often jailed blacks who expressed dissatisfaction with low wages or poor working conditions, and they systematically assisted local leaders in repressing black desires for equality and greater freedom. When black residents protested, they were placed in county jails, where they were incarcerated and often beaten until they agreed to return to work or to conform to local customs.

As a backlash against the economic, political, and cultural changes that were sweeping across the South, a resurgence in the Ku Klux Klan also occurred. Many native whites resented the transformation that was taking place and in their frustration often lashed out at blacks. Klan leaders and their allies in Brevard and Orange counties, for example, murdered Harry T. Moore, state leader of the NAACP, and his wife in their home on Christmas Eve 1950, for conducting a statewide campaign to register blacks to vote in Florida during the late 1940s. Governor Warren reflected the state's racial mores by ignoring this and other acts of violence and intimidation against black citizens and NAACP activists. An FBI-led inquiry into Moore's death found that a widespread network of local officials, police, and militant whites operated throughout central Florida to suppress the rights of blacks. But no legal action was ever taken against any official, and Moore's killers never went to trial.

Nevertheless, the efforts of state political leaders and local officials to control the racial situation were gradually undermined by their own efforts to diversify the state's economy and increase its population. Beginning with its decision against the southern white primary in 1944, the Supreme Court slowly dismantled the legal basis upon which segregation had been built. In Florida, the court's decisions were indirectly supported by the state's newer inhabitants. Business leaders and residents who came predominantly from the Northeast and Midwest had no desire to see their interests jeopardized by a commitment to a long-dead southern past. They insisted that their businesses needed a stable environment in order to prosper. Thus the battle lines were drawn between proponents of traditional southern values and those who sought to build a "new" Florida. Ironically, the notion that "we have seen the enemy and he is us" was especially true in Florida at this time, with racial and social traditions being steadily eroded by policies emphasizing economic development and population growth—policies supported by the same folks who would have preferred to retain segregation.

By the 1950s, the issues of race and reapportionment were inextricably linked. Legislative leaders from north Florida understood that south Floridians did not share their commitment to the state's racial traditions and that residents of the southern region would readily cast tradition aside if their economic prosperity and well-being were threatened. The war over reapportionment thus had great significance.

As the battle unfolded, rural legislators formed the so-called Pork Chop Gang and "took a blood oath to stick together, and did that on all legislation," especially on reapportionment. They did so to preserve Florida's heritage, as they understood it, against the invasion of newcomers. Despite the continued dramatic growth of the state, rural legislators blocked reapportionment, and the legislature remained among the worst apportioned in the nation, with a mere 13.6 percent of the state's population electing more than half of the state senators and only 18 percent of the population electing more than half of the members of the House of Representatives. Governor LeRoy Collins (1955–61), who was elected with the substantial backing of the urban communities of the state, including especially strong support from south Florida, made legislative reapportionment one of his top priorities. He introduced reapportionment in every legislative session during his six years in office, only to see it blocked by rural legislators, who still dominated the Senate leadership and held nearly a majority of the seats in the House.

The battle for control of the legislature and the state took a dramatic turn in the 1950s over the public school desegregation issue. When the Supreme Court announced the *Brown* v. *Board of Education* decision on May 17, 1954, few in Florida were prepared for the ruling. The Pork Chop Gang quickly seized the issue to reassert their political dominance, denouncing the decision and drafting proposals calling for massive resistance against the court-ordered scheme. Representatives from south Florida generally criticized the court's pronouncement as well, but they found themselves and their state being led by north Florida politicians who militantly rejected any compromise on the issue.

Locked in a struggle to win the governorship in a special election at the time of the court's pronouncement, Collins announced his commitment to segregation and said little else. As a southern business progressive, however, Collins was not an extremist. Indeed, he sought to create an environment that would help the state diversify economically and worried that racial militancy would crush his effort to modernize the state. Moreover, as a Florida native, Collins was not anxious to see the ambitions of his state and its future ruined once again. Still, for political reasons he was not prepared to accept desegregation at this point, and he joined with other southern leaders in opposing the *Brown* decision. Richard Kluger noted in his book *Simple Justice* that in 1955 Florida "submitted the most extensive and spirited brief" criticizing the implications of the decision for public education.

Collins's leadership was not as transparent as some northern observers contended, however. While pursuing a variety of measures that were designed to preserve school segregation, he sought simultaneously to avoid racial extremism. Collins well understood that he and Florida moderates had to be exceedingly careful or they would be outmaneuvered by the militants. Indeed, Collins's plan encountered a series of strong challenges from north Florida legislators, who proposed to close down the public schools, commence funding a private school system, and enact an interposition resolution to block implementation of the *Brown* decision. Collins, however, was able to keep the racial militants at bay so that he and Florida gained a reputation for racial moderation. Tourists, new residents, and new businesses continued to stream into the state. Toward the end of his governorship, Collins embarked on a campaign to persuade white Floridians that desegregation was only right and proper and that the state would benefit materially by accepting the change. Although Florida was only one of four southern states with virtually no integration by 1960, the national press portrayed the state as progressive because of Collins's leadership and because his counterparts in Arkansas, Mississippi, and Alabama seemed so extremist by contrast.

Collins also found that he had strong allies for his moderate approach in the business community and among south Floridians in general. Few among the recent arrivals had a personal or economic commitment to segregated schools and a segregated society. It was this attitude that made north Floridians all the more determined to block reapportionment, maintain control of the legislature, preserve their culture, and ensure that Florida would perpetuate segregation. A special legislative committee, created in 1956 and chaired by former governor Charley Johns (1953–55), a resident of Starke, investigated the NAACP as an alleged "communist organization" and sought to ensure conformity of thought in the state's public schools and universities by removing certain textbooks from libraries and classrooms and by firing faculty members.

The efforts of north Floridians to hold on to the reins of power came to an end in the 1960s but not without a last-ditch attempt to retain political control. Although the state lost the political skill of LeRoy Collins, it continued to be a seedbed of change as a result of its massive population growth, a burgeoning tourist economy, and an expanding civil rights movement. After Collins, Florida elected Farris Bryant (1961–65) and Haydon Burns (1965–67) to the governorship. Both were closely allied with conservative elements in the Democratic Party and worked with rural, north Florida legislators to maintain the racial status quo. Efforts to stymie desegregation took on a harder edge. Both Bryant and Burns mobilized the state police, the National Guard, and other state law enforcement bodies to preserve racial customs amidst local civil rights protests and a campaign conducted by the Reverend Martin Luther King, Jr., and the Southern Christian Leadership Conference (SCLC) in St. Augustine. The resistance of local white leaders in St. Augustine to SCLC's civil rights campaign underscored Collins's contention that racism would only polarize Floridians and hurt the state's economic development. In the wake of the King-led campaign, St. Augustine saw its tourism industry decimated, and few celebrated the community's 400th anniversary in 1965. Florida's reputation for racial moderation, which Collins had worked so hard to build, suffered greatly during the first half of the 1960s.

Still, while Governors Bryant and Burns fought to block school desegregation, they simultaneously led efforts to recruit new businesses, and these businesses insisted upon stability. For example, Burns coordinated the recruitment of the Walt Disney Corporation to Orlando in 1965. Disney and the other tourist companies that followed did a great deal to undermine racial extremism and the social instability that accompanied it. In conversations with political leaders, Disney officials emphasized the need for a tranquil environment in order to encourage visitors into the state. They were not advocates for racial change, but they pointed out that racial violence and social instability hurt tourism and harmed the state economically. Racial unrest in Little Rock, Arkansas, and in St. Augustine had devastated both economies. Disney and other executives had no interest in seeing a repeat of that performance in central Florida.

Although Florida's economic development program steadily eroded its commitment to a segregated past, there was no clear sign that its political leaders were prepared to abandon the state's racial traditions until the federal government intervened. Washington effectively removed the civil rights issue from state control by adopting the Civil Rights Act of 1964 and the Voting Rights Act of 1965. Respectively, these two laws abolished segregation in all areas of public life and ended voting restrictions based on race. In 1967, the Supreme Court further ordered the implementation of the principle of one person, one vote in Florida, and with the stroke of a pen dismantled opposition to reapportionment.

The actions of the federal government and courts ended the rural north's stranglehold over Florida. From the end of Reconstruction through World War II, north Floridians had defined the state's development, its race relations, and its place in the nation, even holding on in the face of massive demographic and economic change. But in the wake of the Supreme Court decisions of the 1960s, the balance of power finally shifted to the high-growth areas of south and central Florida. Florida politics would never be—and indeed could never be—the same again.

# 2 Florida in the Modern Era

The years from 1965 to 2000 witnessed a dramatic transformation in Florida. The social, economic, and political culture of north Florida, which had dominated the state for most of the nineteenth and twentieth centuries, was superseded by central and south Florida. The people who migrated to these areas were from the Northeast and Midwest, and they did not share the social and cultural values of those who resided in north Florida. With the assistance of the federal government and the courts, black Floridians and women also led efforts to undermine the restrictions of southern culture and to facilitate their participation in the political process. In addition, the immigration of people from the Caribbean and Central America increased cultural diversity in Florida.

The variety of cultures and people remade Florida, and in the process, the state's historic political and cultural unity, which had eroded steadily from 1940 to 1960, was permanently shattered. The political culture of Florida felt the effects of these developments and was in turn changed dramatically by them. But these developments that swept the state did not produce unity. Instead, Florida became a state of distinct regions, with political leaders struggling to come to terms with this new and often divided Florida.

## The Constitution of 1968 and the Rise of Two-Party Politics

The racial and electoral changes mandated by the federal government and courts were traumatic for Florida and the South in general, but it was not immediately obvious what consequence they would have for state politics. The state and national reforms, and especially the removal of the race issue from state politics, blew a fresh breeze over the entire region. Without a race-based politics and without a north Florida–dominated legislature, the state began to address important issues that had been largely ignored in the battle over segregation. In the process, voters revisited political loyalties that had gone unchallenged during much of the twentieth century.

The most immediate consequence of these developments involved constitutional revision. In 1965 the state legislature established a Constitution Revision Commission to prepare a draft document for legislative consideration. The governor, speaker of the House, president of the Senate, and chief justice of the State Supreme Court appointed the members of the commission. Few anticipated a serious revision of the 1885 Constitution, since the legislature was still under the control of delegates from north Florida. The commission conducted its deliberations in 1966 and prepared a document for submission to the legislature in 1967, when the U.S. Supreme Court intervened. In 1962, the court had ruled in *Baker* v. *Carr* that the apportionment provisions of state constitutions that did not conform to "one man, one vote" were unconstitutional. Because Florida had one of the worst-apportioned legislatures in the nation, the meaning of the law for the state was quite clear. By January 1967, however, the north Florida–dominated legislature had made only minor changes to conform to the 1962 decision. At that point the U.S. Supreme Court explicitly declared in *Swann* v. *Adams* that the apportionment provisions of Florida's Constitution of 1885 were unconstitutional. The court ordered new elections reflecting a more representative apportionment formula.

The *Swann* decision and a new apportionment plan drafted by political scientist Manning Dauer of the University of Florida led to a new legislature that had a remarkably different cast. Representatives from the southern region of the state and from the state's urban centers now held clear majorities in both houses, and the leadership came from that region as well. Suddenly, revision of the Constitution was a matter for serious discussion, with most members of the new majority viewing the 1885 Constitution as an outmoded relic of the Old South.

The new governor, Claude Kirk (1967–71), the first Republican governor in Florida in the twentieth century, also strongly endorsed revision of the Constitution. Kirk felt that by championing revision the Republican Party could enhance its reputation as a proponent of modernization and democratic reform in Florida. Moreover, most of Kirk's electoral support came from central and south Florida, where opposition to the Constitution of 1885 was strongest. To secure adoption, Kirk called three special sessions of the legislature, overriding objections from north Florida legislators. Despite the intense but weak opposition, most Democrats in both houses favored the new Constitution. Even north Florida political leaders had come to recognize that constitutional change was inevitable. In July 1968, legislators overwhelmingly approved the new document, and voters ratified it in November 1968.

The 1968 Constitution represented a substantial revision of the 1885 document. In Article I, it provided a state Bill of Rights, which included provisions for freedom of speech, equal protection of the laws, right to trial by jury, freedom of worship, and other civil liberties that were fairly traditional in the United States. The only controversial section of Article I provided "freedom of choice" in labor contracts. This "right-to-work" provision (found in constitutions throughout the South) required a business to be open to nonunion employees even if it was unionized. Labor has loudly condemned such "right-to-work" provisions as antiunion but has been unsuccessful in repealing them.

Article II of the 1968 Constitution dealt with such routine matters as state boundaries, but section 7 gave the state legislature power to enact laws to protect natural resources and the environment. Florida is one of fewer than ten states that has such a provision in its Constitution. This section reflected both the public and legislature's growing appreciation of the fragile nature of the state's ecology and environment and its importance to economic development. To promote integrity in the political process, Section 8 of Article II called for fiscal disclosure by all public officials in Florida.

Articles III and IV redefined the powers of the legislature and the governor's office. Article III established a bicameral legislature and continued Florida's tradition of having senators serve four-year terms and representatives two-year terms. Article IV significantly strengthened the hand of the governorship by allowing governors to serve two consecutive terms and also making individuals eligible for reelection as governor after sitting out a term. Sections 2 and 3 of Article IV created the office of lieutenant governor (which had been abolished in the 1885 Constitution) and established the lieutenant governor as next in line of succession. Perhaps more significantly, the lieutenant governor ran on the same ticket as the governor and, as the governor's choice, could be relied on to assist him in the many responsibilities of the office. The political ties between the governor and lieutenant governor stood in stark contrast to the governor's relationship with cabinet members, who remained independent.

Despite the changes wrought by the 1968 Constitution, it retained the state's unique cabinet system, reflecting voter and legislative suspicion of executive leadership. This mistrust was rooted in public dissatisfaction with President Lyndon Johnson's leadership in domestic and foreign affairs, especially concerning the Vietnam conflict. There may someday be an opportunity to revamp the cabinet system in Florida and strengthen the power of the governor, but the late 1960s was not that time. The public's hostility to executive leadership had seldom been more profound than in the late 1960s.

The 1968 Constitution did mandate a reorganization and consolidation of the 200-plus state agencies. In response to this edict, in 1969 the legislature approved a major reorganization act collapsing 200 agencies to twenty-two and giving the governor control over half of them. The governor now possessed administrative authority in areas where before he had none.

Even with these changes, however, the executive branch of government remained atomized. By 1990, Florida's executive branch consisted of fourteen agencies under the authority of the governor, six agencies operating under the governor and cabinet, and three constitutional agencies. The governor still presided at weekly cabinet meetings and had a vote only equal to the six elected cabinet members. In addition, the governor served as chairman of a number of boards and commissions, again in which a cabinet officer's vote was equal to the governor's. This collegial form of government makes Florida unique among the fifty states and a source of considerable frustration for state governors.

Article V provided for the state judiciary and remained unchanged from the 1885 Constitution. Many Floridians, however, grew unhappy with the convention's failure to modernize the judiciary and to adopt a merit system for the selection of judges. In 1972, the legislature responded to the concerns of the Florida Bar Association and the public by amending the Constitution to establish a system of county and regional trial courts and two levels of appeal courts, and eliminating municipal courts. Article V was further amended in 1976 to provide a merit retention process (often referred to as the Missouri Plan) for the selection and certifying of appellate judges. Under this system, the governor, consulting a list of qualified candidates who have been screened and approved by a judicial nominating commission, appoints members to the State Supreme Court and to the Courts of Appeal for six-year terms. After six years, the judge's names are placed on ballots and the voters determine whether they should be retained for another six years. No candidate runs in opposition to the serving judge. This plan was designed to ensure that only qualified candidates serve on the courts, that judicial elections do not become personality contests but remain public reviews of a judge's record, and that judgeships should not be treated as the spoils of a partisan contest. In 1978, however, Florida voters rejected an effort to extend merit retention to trial judges.

Articles VI and VII of the 1968 Constitution pertained to suffrage, elections, and state finance. Reflecting the civil rights reforms of the 1960s, Article VI eliminated discrimination in suffrage and elections on the basis of race and gender. This provision also declared that only those twenty-one and older could vote, but it has since been superceded by Amendment 26 to the U.S. Constitution, which reduced the voting age to eighteen. Article VII required the state to balance its budget annually, with the exception of revenue bonds for constructing roads or schools, which could be paid over time. Limits were also placed on the taxing authority of local governments. A ten-mill property tax limit was set on all local government units, reflecting the antitax mentality that has dominated Florida politics throughout the twentieth century. Equally significant, the Constitution prohibited a state income tax.

Article VIII established the parameters of local government and granted limited "home rule" to cities and counties. The 1885 Constitution had carefully restricted local governments to activities specifically authorized by the state legislature. This limitation worked fine when Florida was a small, rural state, but it proved extremely burdensome to communities in the post-1960 era. The 1968 Constitution permitted cities and counties to take any action not specifically prohibited by the Constitution or by state law. This provision freed the cities to address local problems, but the legislature refused to grant cities and counties home rule on matters of taxation. While local governments have property tax authority, they have no other taxing powers independent of state law.

Article IX provided for ways to amend the Constitution. One of the more dramatic political developments pertaining to Article IX in the 1990s was the use of initiative petitions to limit the power of state government. To get a petition on the state ballot, supporters must obtain signatures equivalent to 8 percent of the number of voters in the previous presidential election. This number must also be equal to 8 percent of the voters in at least half of the congressional districts in Florida. The signatures must be verified and submitted ninety days before the general election, and the petition requires a voting majority to pass. Prior to the 1990s, only the supporters of casino gambling in Florida brought such a petition before state voters. Governor Reubin Askew successfully campaigned to defeat the casino gambling measure by persuading voters that casino gambling was inconsistent with the state's commitment to family-oriented tourism.

Beginning in the 1990s, antitax and antigovernment forces, inspired by petition drives in California and by the presidential candidacy of H. Ross Perot, initiated numerous petitions to reduce the size of government in Florida by limiting its taxing authority. The result has enabled a small minority of voters, who sign such petitions and who participate in these elections, to curtail the authority of state legislators and governors, who more properly represent the interests of the state and the needs of its people. These petition drives have affected the direction of state policy, often without the benefit of a deliberative process. By 1997, twenty-nine such initiatives, embracing such arcane subjects as dentures and the establishment of Confederate Memorial Day as a paid state holiday, were gathering signatures.

While overall the new Constitution appeared to enhance the power of the governor, the near simultaneous passage of the Legislative Reorganization Act of 1969 counterbalanced this by significantly strengthening the state legislature. The act reflected the professional, business-oriented philosophy of urban Florida. It mandated annual (as opposed to biennial) meetings of the legislature and created a permanent legislative staff. The Florida legislature almost overnight became a full-time professional body. With experts to guide them, legislators were no longer dependent on the governor and his staff for information on the budget, revenue income, and state spending. Along with the failure of the Constitution of 1968 to reform the cabinet system, the Legislative Reorganization Act made the legislature a major force in Florida politics in the last quarter of the twentieth century.

## The Modernization of Florida and Its Consequence for State Government and Politics

Florida's demographics continued to change dramatically in the post-1960 period, with nearly 700 people a day arriving in the state throughout the 1960s and 1970s. Florida rapidly became the largest and most urbanized state in the South, and its rate of growth in the post–World War II period has been matched by only a handful of states in the nation. In the process, Florida's demographics began to resemble those of the Sunbelt states of Texas, Arizona, and California more than its traditional neighbors in the South. By the 1990s, a majority of Floridians had been born somewhere else. In fact, the number of Florida residents born in New York now exceeds the number who are of southern origin. As a consequence, Florida's economy has felt the dramatic effects of this population growth, becoming increasingly dependent on housing construction, high technology manufacturing, and tourism. The phosphate industry, cattle ranching, the sugar industry, and especially agriculture have continued to play important roles in the economy, but their relative influence has declined significantly. The migration of Latin peoples into southeast Florida from Central America and the Caribbean has also expanded the state's influence in the Caribbean basin and Latin America, enabling Miami to become one of the principal banking and financial centers of the region.

Two critical components of Florida's population expansion in the post-1960 era were retired persons and Cuban immigrants. Florida's senior citizens, who constituted 2.4 million people aged sixty-five and over and more than 18 percent of the state's population by 1990—the highest in the United States—have put the brake on government initiatives and social policy. A Republican pollster has observed that since seniors in Florida have already been uprooted once, it becomes very important that they have stability in their new life. "That leads to a drawbridge mentality," he told the *Miami Herald*, "that once they've come here, they don't want anybody else to come along and spoil it." Nevertheless, while pressuring state politicians to limit new tax initiatives and other revenue measures that might adversely affect their fixed incomes, senior citizens have made heavy demands on the state's social and medical services. Thus they support programs to aid the infirm and protect the elderly from crime but generally resist new spending for education, families, and other social programs. Moreover, because the elderly are so well represented by the influential American Association of Retired Persons, and because they tend to vote in much higher percentages than other segments of the population, they have exercised a disproportionate influence on state politics.

Cuban Americans, who fled Communist Cuba in the late 1950s and early 1960s and generally settled in Dade County, made a rapid and remarkably successful adjustment to American life. Along with federal assistance programs, their emerging middle-class wealth and sheer size (nearly 700,000 in south Florida) have facilitated their economic advancement and their adjustment to American society. They quickly became a powerful political force in Dade County and Florida in general. Because of their opposition to Castro and communism, Cuban Americans have focused their attention primarily on foreign affairs, but they have also been strong advocates of unfettered American capitalism, which has served them well. Beyond these political priorities, they have generally been conservative on social programs and on issues of race, reflecting their Roman Catholicism and their focus on community needs and concerns.

The Cuban community adds a further ethnic dynamic to Florida politics. Cubans often imitate the ethnic activism of Jewish Floridians, who have actively pursued support for Israel throughout its existence. This ethnic dynamic has in turn marginalized the racial concerns that dominated Florida for much of the nineteenth and twentieth centuries. Florida's Cubans have voted in larger numbers than black Floridians, and their political involvement has given them a more influential voice in state politics than their black counterparts.

The Republican Party, which made slow but steady gains in the postwar period, benefited considerably from the growing number of senior citizens and Cubans. In addition, Florida's latent Republicanism in national elections gradually began to make itself felt in state politics. From 1952 on, Floridians voted for Republican presidential candidates in every election but 1964, 1976, and 1996, when they cast their ballots for native southerners Lyndon Johnson, Jimmy Carter, and Bill Clinton. Much of this animus to Democratic presidential candidates reflected voter anger over the party's support for desegregation and social reform in the 1950s and 1960s and over the creation of the social welfare state in the late 1960s.

Prior to the 1960s, Republicans posed little threat to most Democratic candidates. In his campaign for governor in 1954, LeRoy Collins spent only $174.00 to defeat his Republican opponent with over 80 percent of the vote. In 1960, George Smathers won a U.S. Senate seat with more than 76 percent of the popular vote. Thus, despite the popularity of Republican presidential candidates in Florida, state voters had yet to show much enthusiasm for Republican candidates in state races.

All that changed in the 1960s, with the stunning gubernatorial victory of Claude Kirk in 1966 and Edward Gurney's defeat of former governor LeRoy Collins for the U.S. Senate in 1968. Both victories resulted from the expansion of an electorate that was not committed through racial or historical ties to the Democratic Party and by widespread dissatisfaction of native Floridians with President Lyndon Johnson's Great Society programs. In the first effective statewide media campaigns, Kirk in 1966 and Gurney in 1968 characterized their opponents in thirty-second television spots as liberal, free-spending Democrats. Gurney interjected references to "liberal LeRoy" Collins in every speech. He and Kirk accused their Democratic rivals of holding political views that were inconsistent with the interests of Floridians, a charge that would lead state Democrats to begin distancing themselves from the national Democratic Party.

The 1966 and 1968 elections signaled that Floridians were no longer content with the state Democratic Party, but they did not signal the beginning of a stampede toward the Republicans. But the "Grand Old Party" had indeed suddenly become a viable political alternative, however—something it had never been in Florida since the end of Reconstruction. Although the elections of Kirk and Gurney had more do with voter reaction to President Johnson, the national Democratic Party, and the social revolution of the 1960s, voters perceived Republicans Kirk and Gurney as more likely to preserve traditional state social and political values than their Democratic opponents. Yet evidence of the continuing dominance of the Democratic Party could be found in the distribution of filing fees for state offices. In 1972 the Democratic Party received $600,000 in fees, while the Republican Party, with few state candidates, received almost nothing.

As state Democrats separated themselves from the national party and reasserted values with which Floridians were more comfortable, the Republican's success fizzled. Kirk, who revealed a talent for what many viewed as bizarre and inappropriate behavior, and Gurney, who was indicted on bribery and conspiracy charges (but found not guilty), aided the Democrats' revival. Kirk especially alienated voters with his histrionics on everything from his seizure of the Manatee County schools to block a federal court order requiring busing to achieve desegregation to

Fred Cone was inaugurated as governor in 1937. His approach to the depression was to balance the budget and cut spending. He had no understanding of or sympathy with deficit spending or with the New Deal's programs such as the Works Progress Administration and, in fact, felt that they damaged the country. (Florida State Archives)

Governor Fred P. Cone appeared with Senator Claude Pepper in the late 1930s the two representing the political extremes in Florida. Cone, a political and fiscal conservative, cut the state budget dramatically during the depression. He detested the philosophy behind the New Deal and refused to provide state matching funds for federal programs. President Roosevelt's New Deal programs saved the state and many of its citizens during this period, and Pepper was one of its most ardent supporters. (Florida State Archives)

Marion Post, photographer for the Farm Security Administration, captured the mood among black Floridians in the Great Depression in 1941. Although the war in Europe and Asia soon engulfed the United States and ended the depression, no help seemed in sight for these black men when this picture was taken. (Library of Congress, Farm Security Administration)

Governor Spessard Holland taking the oath of office from Chief Justice Glenn Terrell of the Florida Supreme Court in 1941. Holland's term was consumed by the events of World War II, the defense of Florida's long coastline from German incursion, and the utilization of the state for military training. (P. K. Yonge Library of Florida History)

World War II changed Florida forever. The military used significant parts of Florida for training and helped develop the state in the process. During 1942–43 servicemen trained along the beach, in this case with gas masks. The Army Air Force occupied 70,000 hotel rooms along the beach in 1942. (Florida State Archives)

Army Air Force trainees marched to their classroom on Miami Beach. Many of the servicemen returned to Florida after the war to spur its population explosion in the postwar era. (Florida State Archives)

(*Left to right*): Vice President Alben Barkley joined University of Florida President J. Hillis Miller, Senator Claude Pepper, Governor Fuller Warren, and Senator Spessard Holland at homecoming at the University of Florida in 1949. Because many of the state's leaders had attended and graduated from the University of Florida, this weekend became a time for political leaders to gather and interact. (P. K. Yonge Library of Florida History)

(*Left to right*): Senator Claude Pepper, Governor Millard Caldwell, and Senator Spessard Holland posed beside one of Florida's colossal banyan trees. Caldwell and Holland represented the political mainstream in Florida and sought to modernize the state while maintaining a small government structure and the political status quo. Pepper remained an avid New Dealer in the postwar era and championed the needs of the common man and an activist approach to government. (P. K. Yonge Library of Florida History)

## "DISGRACE TO SENATE" ... AND FLORIDA.

THIS IS NO PLACE FOR POLITICS

PEPPER

Reproduced by Permission of The Sunday Star, Washington, D. C.

This typical cartoon and hundreds of editorials denounced Claude Pepper, NOT a veteran despite his printed claims, the last time he injected a sordid note on the Service issue, with his infamous untruth: "It was the workers' sons who died on the battlefields while the sons of manufacturers stayed home and got rich," which Pepper shouted in February, 1949, at Senate Committee hearings on the Taft-Hartley Act. His target then was Ira Mosher, a prominent executive, whose answer was crushing in its simple sadness: "I lost three in my family during the war." Today, Pepper's vicious attacks on the honorable war record of his U.S. Senatorial opponent, Congressman George Smathers, have boomeranged and spotlighted his own avoidance of two World Wars. In contrast, George Smathers left his draft-exempt position, enlisted, and served 39 months with the U.S. Marines, 17 of them in the Pacific War Theater.

The 1950 U.S. senatorial primary was one of the most bruising campaigns in Florida history. George Smathers accused incumbent Claude Pepper of being sympathetic to the communists and of lying to the public about his war record, but Pepper captured over 45 percent of the vote against the handsome, popular, and personable Smathers, who was, in fact, a veteran of the war in the Pacific. (P. K. Yonge Library of Florida History)

Florida received a $2 million check from the federal government to create Everglades National Park. Senator Spessard Holland (*far left*) and Senator Claude Pepper (*standing behind the seated man*) were instrumental in gaining President Harry Truman's support for the park. Governor Millard Caldwell stood second from the right. Throughout the postwar period, Florida struggled to maintain a balance between its delicate environment and the pressures of development. (Florida State Archives)

Charley Johns, who had been president of the Florida Senate, became governor when Dan McCarty died suddenly in office in 1953. When the Florida Supreme Court announced a special election to be held in 1954 to replace McCarty, Johns, a leading member of the Pork Chop Gang in north Florida, announced his candidacy, as did State Senator LeRoy Collins, a close friend and ally of McCarty. Collins won easily and kept the Pork Choppers from controlling the governorship and state politics during the years of desegregation. (P. K. Yonge Library of Florida History)

**LeRoy
COLLINS**

**Farris
BRYANT**

**Fuller
WARREN**

## SUMTER L.
# LOWRY

## THE POLITICAL LAWYER CANDIDATES

*A VOTE FOR ANY ONE OF THESE . . .
IS A VOTE FOR*

# RACE MIXING!

**EXPERIENCED BUSINESSMAN**

*A VOTE FOR LOWRY IS
A VOTE TO KEEP*

## WHITE SCHOOLS WHITE

# PROTECT

- THE SOVEREIGNTY OF THE STATE OF FLORIDA
- THE OPPORTUNITY AND SOUND DEVELOPMENT OF FLORIDA
- YOUR SOCIAL AND ECONOMIC WELFARE
- YOUR CHILDREN'S FUTURE

*Vote for* - **SUMTER L. LOWRY** *and -*
# KEEP WHITE SCHOOLS WHITE

### LOWRY for GOVERNOR
CAMPAIGN COMMITTEE
504 O'REILLY BUILDING
JACKSONVILLE 2, FLORIDA

BULK RATE
U. S. POSTAGE
**PAID**
Jacksonville, Florida
Permit No. 2219

# Rural Box Holder
# Local

20

**SUMTER L. LOWRY
CANDIDATE FOR GOVERNOR** **THE TRUTH** ABOUT THE FOUR MAJOR CANDIDATES **FOR GOVERNOR**

In the state Democratic primary of 1956, three candidates vied with Governor LeRoy Collins for the governorship. Collins was ruled eligible for reelection by the Supreme Court because he had served only the last two years of McCarty's term. The *Brown* decision of 1954 ordering school desegregation had become a major issue in the state by 1956. The three candidates challenging Collins used the race issue; the most extreme of them was Sumter Lowry. Collins won and ensured that Florida would pursue a moderate course of action in the battle over desegregation. (P. K. Yonge Library of Florida History)

Return

# FULLER
# WARREN

*YOUR*

# GOVERNOR

STATE OF FLORIDA )
                 } ss  A F F I D A V I T
COUNTY OF DADE   )

    Before the undersigned authority person-
ally appeared FULLER WARREN, who, being duly
sworn, says on oath:

    That no Negroes will be admitted to White
schools and colleges of this state if Fuller
Warren is governor.

Subscribed and sworn
to before me this 23rd
day of April, 1956.

Fuller Warren

Notary Public, State of Florida at large
My commission expires Dec. 26, 1959
Bonded by Mass. Bonding & Insurance Co.

Notary Public

A poster on behalf of the candidacy of Fuller Warren for governor in 1956 included an affidavit in which he pledged to maintain segregation in Florida's
schools and colleges. (P. K. Yonge Library of Florida History)

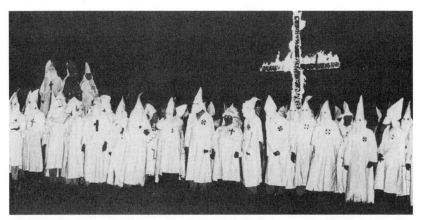

The Ku Klux Klan operated actively throughout much of Florida during the first half of the twentieth century, often with the support of members of the local police and sheriff's departments. Together, the Klan and the police enforced traditional racial customs against black residents. (Florida State Archives)

(*Left to right*): Senator George Smathers, Senator Spessard Holland, and Governor LeRoy Collins attended a rally for Democratic presidential candidate Adlai Stevenson in 1956. Despite the support of Florida's three leading politicians, Florida cast its votes for the incumbent president, Dwight David Eisenhower, and continued a trend of voting for Republican presidents while retaining Democratic leadership at the state level. Florida has voted for only three Democratic presidential candidates since 1952—Lyndon Johnson, Jimmy Carter, and Bill Clinton, all southerners. (P. K. Yonge Library of Florida History)

Governor LeRoy Collins met with Seminole Indians at the governor's mansion in Tallahassee in 1957. In an effort to promote tolerance, he sought to increase understanding among Floridians about their unique history and about the diversity of its population. (Florida State Archives)

LeRoy Collins (*center*) talking with President John Kennedy and Senator George Smathers. After a remarkable six years as Florida's governor, Collins became president of the National Association of Broadcasters. President Lyndon Johnson subsequently appointed him as the first director of the Community Relations Service in 1964 and then as secretary of commerce. Kennedy and Smathers were close friends, and their escapades would ultimately damage the reputations of both men. (Florida State Archives)

*Opposite:* President John Kennedy and Senator Spessard Holland, governor of Florida in 1941–45 and U.S. Senator in 1947–71, gathered for the Orange Bowl game in Miami in January 1963. Florida had not voted for Kennedy in 1960, and both he and Holland were anxious to reverse that vote in 1964. Sadly, the president was assassinated in November 1963. (Florida State Archives)

The "Bloomer Lady," Mrs. Nell Foster Rogers, lobbied the legislature and governor's office on behalf of the public interest between 1947 and 1973 and became something of an institution in Tallahassee with her corduroy shirt, lisle hose, and broad-brimmed straw hat. (Florida State Archives)

his use of a private corporation to wage war on crime in Florida. When he raised $300,000 to cover personal expenses, conducted a personal relationship with an unknown "Madame X," and threw lavish parties for friends and supporters, the voters had enough.

In 1970, Democratic Party leaders set aside individual ambition to rally behind Reubin Askew for governor and Lawton Chiles for the U.S. Senate. Reflecting the emergence of a new Democratic Party in Florida, Askew and Chiles would go on to become two of the most prominent figures in Florida political history. In 1970 they had the job of stanching the bleeding in the Democratic Party and returning it to the governor's mansion and the Senate. Askew easily defeated Kirk with 57 percent of the vote and in the process persuaded Floridians that his brand of Democratic leadership offered voters a more constructive approach to addressing state needs than that provided by Kirk and the Republicans. Perhaps more significantly, Chiles captured 54 percent of the vote in defeating William Cramer. Known as Mr. Republican, Cramer had been the first member of his party to be elected to Congress (1954) from Florida in the twentieth century and was well respected throughout the state. Aided by the unpopularity of Kirk, Askew and Chiles built a successful coalition of voters from south and north Florida and the Panhandle. It was this coalition, along with the achievements of Askew and Chiles, that enabled Democrats to reassert their control of state politics from 1970 to the mid-1980s.

During his campaign, Chiles launched a new kind of strategy to emphasize the democratic commitment of his candidacy. By 1970, television had already come to dominate and distort political campaigns, during which voters often caught a glimpse of the candidates only in highly staged thirty- or sixty-second segments. Chiles sought to bypass television by walking all the way across the state, meeting directly with voters on the way. It was a gimmick that resonated well with Floridians who wanted more than cardboard cutouts as candidates. Bob Graham, who succeeded Reubin Askew as governor, mimicked Chiles by spending a hundred days during his campaign in 1978 working alongside voters at various jobs around the state. Graham's technique, like Chiles's, revitalized voter interest in the Democratic Party and allowed it to claim that it was the party of the people. By placing its major candidates in direct contact with voters, party leaders had also developed a statewide strategy that overcame the difficulties of Florida's geography and diversity.

The inability of the Republican Party to capitalize on its successes in the late 1960s resulted from the Democratic counterattack and the absence of a solid foundation upon which to challenge Democrats over the long term. Republican voter registration in the state was less than half that for Democrats, and the party had difficulty finding candidates to challenge for many state and local offices. Moreover, the sullied reputations of Kirk and Gurney mirrored Republican president Richard Nixon's loss of popularity during the Watergate crisis. Thus, despite signs of promise, the Republican Party found itself saddled with the reputation that it "could not govern straight." By 1979, the Republicans held no statewide political office and could claim only 26 percent of the seats in the state legislature and only three of fifteen congressional seats. But Democrats could take little consolation with these developments, because philosophically many Florida voters were still at odds with the national Democratic Party on many issues, and many of the state's new voters were identifying with the Republican Party. Given this volatile situation, it would only be a matter of time before the Republicans mounted a more serious and systematic challenge to state Democratic leadership.

## Florida at the End of the Twentieth Century

The demise of race as an issue in Florida politics and the reapportionment of the state legislature in the late 1960s enabled voters and political leaders to focus on issues that had long gone unattended. Despite the bumptious nature of his governorship, Claude Kirk reawakened Floridians to the fragile nature of its environment and led an effort to stop the construction of the Cross-Florida Barge Canal. Proposed in order to link east and west Florida commercially and to establish Florida as a hub for sea traffic passing from the Gulf of Mexico to the Atlantic and back, the canal quickly lost support when Floridians became aware of the potential damage to drinking and recreational waters if a major shipping accident occurred. Kirk's leadership proved important in convincing fellow Republicans and President Nixon to throw the White House's support behind the anticanal effort.

Kirk's campaign against the canal reflected the emergence of an environmental movement in Florida, which owed much of its support to the political activism of women and the increasing prominence of south Florida in state politics. Often relegated to the netherworld of Florida politics, women struggled to find a place in what had been traditionally viewed as the domain of men. In the "good old boy" world of Florida politics, family issues and education were among the few public realms in which women's participation was deemed socially appropriate. But this was not sufficient for many women, and some, like May Mann Jennings (a pioneer supporter of women's and environmental issues throughout most of the twentieth century), Marjory Stoneman Douglas, and Marjorie Carr, spoke out against the degradation of Florida's environment by business interests. These women set the stage for the emergence of such prominent political leaders as Gwen Margolis and Toni Jennings, both of whom served as president of the Florida Senate, and Betty Castor, who as commissioner of education became the first woman elected to the state cabinet. In their writings and public addresses, these women provided the impetus for the environmental movement in the state and, in the process, gave women an important voice in state politics.

Under the laissez-faire approach of Florida's traditional north Florida political leaders, south Florida's environment suffered most, as unrestricted growth jeopardized its supply of fresh water, its wildlife, its beaches, and the general quality of life. Spurred on by Douglas and Carr, environmental politics reached its apogee under Governor Reubin Askew (1971–79). Askew feared that Florida, like California, was in "great danger" of becoming a "paradise lost." He launched his environmental campaign at a conference on water and land management in September 1971. From this conference came the Environmental Land and Water Management Act, the Water Resources Act, and the State Comprehensive Planning Act in 1972, which together provided the framework for state development and environmental protection in subsequent years. Under Askew, Florida also began a land acquisition program to preserve some of its most sensitive and endangered environments.

A "nondrinking, nonsmoking Presbyterian elder" who took his religion and governmental responsibilities seriously, Askew provided Florida with gubernatorial leadership that had not been seen since LeRoy Collins in the 1950s. This in turn gave the state Democratic Party a new lease on life. During his terms as governor, Askew called not only for environmental reform but also for tax reform, facilitation of public school integration, the adoption of a corporate income tax, financial disclosure by public officials, and "government in the sunshine." When the legislature showed little interest in his proposals, Askew took them directly to the voters. In a series of referenda, he persuaded Floridians to adopt a corporate income tax, to support a "sunshine law," and to reject casino gambling. Worried about mounting public criticism of politicians, Askew sought to put into place a framework that would ensure openness and honesty in the conduct of public business. While the openness in government that was required by the sunshine law certainly helped, it did not halt public cynicism over politics. Askew enjoyed voter respect and confidence, but few others could command such loyalty.

After Askew's two terms as governor, the reigns of state power passed to Bob Graham (1979–87), Askew's close friend and ally and a state senator from Dade County. Graham built upon the electoral coalition that Askew and Chiles had developed, in particular expanding Askew's environmental initiatives through promotional campaigns known as "Save Our Everglades" and "Save Our Coastline." Styling himself as the "education governor," Graham also sought to strengthen public and university education in order to broaden opportunities for Floridians and enhance business recruitment efforts. Graham's approach to educational reform was not new, and he was especially indebted to the proposals of Governors Caldwell and Collins before him, but Graham proved to be an unusually effective spokesman for education, gaining support among both conservative and progressive members of the legislature by linking education to economic development.

Democratic unity, which Graham had been instrumental in maintaining and which had reestablished party leadership in the state, began to crumble again in the 1980s. Individual ambitions became increasingly difficult to restrain for the good of the party, especially with Republicans offering little substantial opposition in gubernatorial or senatorial contests. The Democratic Party primary became a contest among ambitious individuals. In the Democratic primary for the U.S. Senate in 1980, for example, multiple candidates campaigned for the nomination, and the incumbent senator Richard Stone lost in a bitterly fought contest to State Insurance Commissioner Bill Gunter. In the general election, Stone refused to campaign for Gunter against Republican Paula Hawkins. Although Hawkins had little statewide reputation, she was bolstered by a united Republican Party, the growing prominence of women in state and national politics, by a personal reputation for civic responsibility, and by Ronald Reagan, the Republican candidate for president, who proved enormously popular in Florida. In a stunning upset, Hawkins defeated Gunter for the U.S. Senate and became the first and only women so far to hold this office in Florida.

In 1986, as they prepared for the gubernatorial contest to replace Graham, Democrats were again sharply divided. After a particularly intense Democratic primary, the defeated candidate for the nomination, Attorney General Jim Smith, refused to support nominee Steve Pajcic in the general election. Behind a unified Republican organization and with the support of President Reagan, Tampa mayor Bob Martinez easily captured the governor's office and became Florida's second Republican governor in the twentieth century.

As personal ambitions began to eat away at the their party's position of leadership, Democrats also faced the challenge of a reinvigorated Republican Party under the leadership of President Ronald Reagan. State Republicans eagerly embraced Reagan and sought to rebuild the party around his policies. Reagan's personal style as well as his conservative domestic and foreign policy initiatives enjoyed an enormous following among Floridians and southerners generally. His denunciation of the "bloated" federal bureaucracy and his proposals for slashing taxes and reducing government spending found widespread support in a state where small government and low taxes had long been a fixture of political life.

Reagan's popularity in Florida sparked a dramatic expansion in Republican voter registration. Fed initially by voters in their twenties and thirties, the state Republican Party also gained support among senior citizens and residents of north Florida. Thus, Republican support was no longer confined to the "golden horseshoe" from West Palm Beach on the southeast coast, to Orlando, and on to St. Petersburg and Naples on the southwest coast. Indeed, Republicans could now be found in every region of Florida. As evidence of this deepening support, by the mid-1980s Republicans were able to challenge Democratic candidates at all levels of government. Among the most notable victories for the Reagan revolution in Florida were Bob Martinez's gubernatorial victory in 1986 and Connie Mack's senatorial win in 1988. Mack in particular gave the party the political skill and leadership that it had been lacking in its statewide leaders. The party's new strength was demonstrated further by the distribution of state filing fees in 1988: Republicans received $343,066, just behind the $397,873 given to the Democrats.

The mounting rivalry between the parties dramatically escalated the costs of running for statewide office. Expenditures for the 1986 senatorial campaign between Bob Graham and Paula Hawkins totaled $13.2 million, and the gubernatorial campaign in 1990 cost nearly $16 million. The 1994 gubernatorial campaign exceeded all previous highs, with Lawton Chiles and Jeb Bush raising over $17.5 million and spending most of that money in a blistering campaign. Despite a 1973 state law limiting contributions to $3,000 for each election, campaign coffers bloated to the point where they offended many Floridians. In the 1990 governor's race, Democrat Lawton Chiles appealed to the public's disillusionment by limiting contributions to his campaign to $100.00. He received more than 75,000 contributions, a record for a state campaign in Florida, and, more important, seized control of an issue that ultimately carried him to victory over incumbent governor Martinez.

By the late 1980s the Republican Party had achieved a depth and maturity in its leadership that enabled it to compete for most offices in

Florida, but it still suffered from a general lack of experience and political sophistication. Questions about the party's ability to govern persisted. In 1987, for example, Governor Bob Martinez brought in many Republicans to replace Democrats in state office, which was not unusual or inappropriate for a new governor. But the number of his appointments and their lack of experience and occasional incompetence gave credence to Democratic charges of "spoils system" politics. Martinez's administration was slow to counter such criticism, which only gave the charges greater merit in the eyes of voters.

This criticism paled next to the firestorm that Martinez's support of a service tax engendered. Amidst concerns that state revenues could not keep up with the demand for basic services, Martinez proposed the service tax to provide the state with needed revenue. The proposal struck many supporters as curious in light of his criticism of gubernatorial opponent Steve Pajcic as a "liberal, free spender." Republicans were particularly perplexed by Martinez's proposal because the national party was simultaneously trying to reduce federal spending and taxes. When state newspapers joined forces with the legal establishment to condemn the proposal because of its impact on business, Martinez suddenly retreated and urged the legislature to repeal the tax. The governor appeared more than indecisive, and his maneuverings crippled his administration at its outset, paving the way for the return of the Democratic Party to the governor's mansion in 1990.

Despite Martinez's reelection defeat, the Republican Party continued to build its base in the state through active registration efforts. A 1998 survey shows Democrats maintaining a slight edge in registered voters, with 45.43 percent as opposed to 40.18 percent for Republicans (registered independents constituted approximately 13 percent; see fig. 2). Democrats could take little satisfaction from these numbers, however, because the gap between registered Democrats and Republicans had declined by 15 percent in just twelve years. Republican growth has been so widespread that by the mid-1990s the party constituted a powerful force even in north Florida, with majorities in Santa Rosa and Okaloosa counties, where earlier generations would have renounced their citizenship before voting Republican. Connie Mack enjoyed such

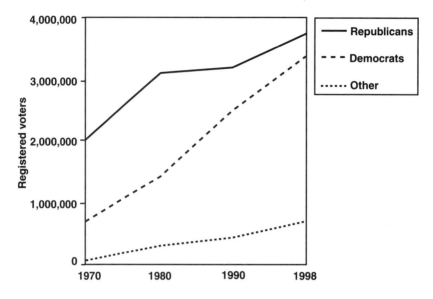

Fig. 2. Registered voters by party, Florida, 1970–1998.

widespread popularity throughout the state that no major Democrat challenged him in 1994, and he won reelection to the Senate with 70 percent of the vote.

To combat the Republican juggernaut, Democrats have had to refine their strategy in statewide elections. Both Governor Chiles and Senator Graham have sought to capture large majorities in Dade and Broward counties, divide voters along the Interstate 4 corridor from Daytona Beach to Tampa, and win in north Florida. The Republican strategy has been essentially the opposite. In particular, party leaders have attempted to limit Democratic majorities in Dade and Broward, capture the I-4 corridor with a sizable majority, and not worry about north Florida.

The coalition between the rural north and the liberal southeast is an odd one in Florida politics. Reubin Askew put these strange bedfellows together in 1970 when he won his first election to the governorship. A native of Pensacola, Askew successfully forged alliances with southeastern liberals on such issues as reapportionment and civil rights. The same coalition elected Lawton Chiles to the U.S. Senate, brought Bob Graham (an urbane Miamian but also a dairy farmer) and Chiles to the governor's mansion, and took Graham from the governor's office to the U.S. Senate. This, too, was the coalition that enabled Jimmy Carter, a southern peanut farmer, and Bill Clinton to carry Florida in the presidential elections of 1976 and 1996.

The simultaneous effort to court voters from the southeast and from north Florida was never more apparent than during the 1994 gubernatorial campaign. Seeking reelection, Governor Chiles, himself a Lakeland businessman and a self-made millionaire, characterized himself as a traditional southerner. In his first debate with Republican candidate Jeb Bush, Chiles told the audience and a perplexed Bush that he spoke "Cracker," and in the last debate he referred to himself as an "old he-coon." These pronouncements did little for his candidacy in the retirement communities of Broward County and the academic communities of Gainesville and Tallahassee. But Chiles had already solidified that support, and he and his aides decided that this very close gubernatorial contest would be decided in Florida's rural heartland.

Despite the political skill of the Democrats, the victory of Chiles in 1994, and the vagaries of Florida voters, the Republican Party appears to be in the process of securing control of state politics. As Florida enters the new millennium, Republicans control the state Senate and the House of Representatives and hold three of the six cabinet offices, thirteen of twenty-one congressional seats, and one of the seats in the U.S. Senate. In 1998, the party had a ten-seat majority in the House and a nine-seat majority in the Senate, which constituted a gain of nine seats in the Senate and twenty-one in the House in just ten years (see table 1). The question of whether the Republican Party will be a long-term factor in Florida politics has been answered. As of this writing, polls suggest as well that in 1998 Jeb Bush will capture the governorship on his second try and that the Republicans will likely strengthen their control over both legislative chambers. Republicans have reason to be wary of such predictions, however. The remarkable success of Bill Clinton's presidential campaign in 1996 suggests that nothing can be certain in Florida politics.

Table 1. Party makeup of the Florida Legislature

| YEAR | SENATE | | HOUSE | |
|------|--------|--------|--------|--------|
| | Dem. | Rep. | Dem. | Rep. |
| 1986 | 25 | 15 | 76 | 44 |
| 1988 | 23 | 17 | 75 | 45 |
| 1990 | 23 | 17 | 74 | 46 |
| 1992 | 20 | 20 | 71 | 49 |
| 1994 | 19 | 21 | 63 | 57 |
| 1996 | 17 | 23 | 59 | 61 |
| 1998 | 16 | 24 | 55 | 65 |

## Viewing the Past and Looking to the Future

The modernization of state government, the abandonment of race and a gerrymandered legislature, and the adoption of the Constitution of 1968 and judicial reform have combined to markedly improve the quality of Florida politics. In little more than three decades, Florida has gone from being a Deep South, largely rural and agricultural state, in which the Democratic Party enjoyed a near monopoly and was committed to segregation, to a large, diverse, and heavily urbanized state in which the two major parties are locked in a titanic struggle for political control.

Even with reforms in the legislature and state bureaucracy and a more competitive political environment, Florida has faced enormous difficulty in addressing its social, educational, health, and safety concerns because it has attracted so many new residents and businesses by offering low taxes, cheap labor, abundant and inexpensive land, and small government. Throughout this recent period, the state has remained a haven for people seeking to avoid paying personal income taxes. A significant number of military personnel, for example, have claimed residence through a post office box in order to enjoy the state's considerable tax advantages. More recently, Florida has become a haven for those declaring personal bankruptcy because its bankruptcy laws are so flexible. These developments have undermined efforts to build a statewide consensus to address current and future needs in a thoughtful manner.

Adding to its inability to build a statewide consensus, Florida remains sharply divided by regions, with local voters showing little or no concern for the rest of the state. Some of this, of course, is due to the constant arrival of new voters, who have little understanding of the needs of the state. But much more of it is due to certain regional dynamics that undermine statewide concerns. In Orange County, for example, residents do not believe they have anything in common with diverse southeast Florida and have no interest in addressing their concerns. They have just as little interest in state government and developments in Tallahassee, because it is a region that is largely self-sufficient and requires little from the state capital. Despite the voters' rejection of all but two tax proposals (a small library tax and a resort tax on tourists) in the last quarter-century, central Florida enjoys huge revenues generated by the 35 million tourists who visit the region annually. Unemployment is virtually unknown in the area. As a result, residents are quite satisfied with their lot.

The consequence of such attitudes has been dramatic. In 1990, for example, Florida ranked last in the nation in spending for social programs, and in 1995 it ranked last in spending for higher education. Two newly constructed prisons remained closed in 1992 because the state lacked the revenue to pay for guards. Like most other states in the mid-1990s, Florida also found itself bedeviled by Medicaid costs, which threatened its long-term financial solvency. The expression "thank God for Mississippi" has often been heard in the state capitol as political leaders watched Florida fall further and further behind the rest of the nation.

Hurricane Andrew, which devastated south Florida in the fall of 1992, suggested that there was trouble in paradise, and the tourist murders in the fall of 1993 seemed to confirm it. These developments not only highlighted, but seemed symptomatic of, the state's worsening social, environmental, and economic problems. By the mid-1990s, crime, poverty, educational concerns, and racial and ethnic tensions all conspired to threaten the quality of life in Florida and to dismantle the Florida dream.

The dream faced further erosion at the hands of the two political parties, which waged war for leadership of the state. The pressures of this battle and the potential stakes involved so politicized the legislative process that the social, environmental, and economic needs of Floridians were often weighed against the political advantages they offered rather than against their importance for the state. It was a political environment that was ill suited to statesmanship and to solving difficult problems.

As Florida enters a new century and a new millennium, it remains fraught with possibilities and problems. The economic boom following the end of the recession in Florida in 1993 sparked a dramatic recovery. The collapse of the Cold War and the explosion of international commerce enabled Florida tourism and trade to reach all-time highs in 1998 and helped shrink unemployment to less than 5 percent. A successful lawsuit brought by the state against the tobacco industry pumped an additional $11.3 billion into the treasury. Suddenly the problems that engulfed the state in 1995 seemed trivial. But Florida's economy continues to rest on a shaky foundation of low-paying service jobs and tourism, and state leaders in both parties have been unable to improve the situation. Moreover, the state's inability to address such fundamental problems as education, quality of life for children, and environmental needs persists.

Florida's sheer size and diversity make it one of a small number of bellwether states in the nation and a potential political and economic leader in the global arena. The traditional southern politics of the state has been replaced by a politics that is much more inclusive and representative, but this transition has not solved all of the state's problems. Tremendous growth has replaced a rural, Deep South identity with no identity at all. Floridians have little sense of themselves as a people, and there exists little in common between those who reside in Key West and those who live in Pensacola. One longtime observer of state politics has commented, "For most Floridians, there is no reason to sublimate their personal interests to the interests of the whole, because they have no sense of what the whole is." The absence of such a statewide identity has limited the ability of its political leaders to address statewide needs. The efforts of Floridians to adjust to their new Florida parallels the experiences of people in other fast growing states. Indeed, it is for this reason that political experts note, "as Florida goes, so goes the South and the Sunbelt."

# 3

## Florida's Government and Administrative Structure

Reflecting the state's southern heritage as well as its rapid population growth and dramatic modernization, Florida's government is a peculiar and often ungainly mix of the old and new. The two state capitol buildings, which sit atop the highest of Tallahassee's seven hills, symbolize this disjuncture between past and present. The tallest, which stands twenty-two stories high, was built in the early 1970s to house the executive branch officers and staff, the House of Representatives, and the Senate. Across a small brick plaza in front of the new capitol is the old capitol building, a three-story structure with tall white columns and canopied windows that dates back to the nineteenth century. It looks like a mansion from the antebellum era. Although the old capitol appears small next to its modern counterpart, it continues to cast a long shadow—literally and figuratively—over the state.

The dominant feature of the past that still weighs heavily on state government is the fragmentation of its executive branch. Throughout the nineteenth century and especially in the decades following Reconstruction, Floridians deliberately limited the authority of the governor. The executive office felt these restrictions most in the twentieth century, when governors tried to address crises created by the Great Depression, World War II, and the massive population growth following the war. Much of the effort to modernize state government in the twentieth century has focused on eliminating fragmentation and establishing mechanisms to strengthen control at the state and local levels of government.

## Development of Florida Government

The most significant advances in the modernization of Florida government occurred in the late 1960s and early 1970s. At the time of these changes, Florida had already become a modern, urban state, but it still had a "horse and buggy" government. The state's population had reached approximately 5 million, but the legislature met only every other year; legislators were elected from large, multimember districts, which limited the voting power of minorities; the state legislature was badly apportioned and unresponsive to urban needs; the governor served for only one term and could not be reelected; and executive authority was scattered among numerous commissions and boards. Florida's ship of state had no rudder.

By 1970, the worst of these problems had been corrected. The federal courts had required the reapportionment of the state legislature, enabling legislators from the large growth areas of Florida to take control of the legislative agenda. This decision, in combination with the adoption of the 1968 Constitution, helped modernize state government. The legislature began meeting annually; representation shifted to small, single-member districts and began to reflect the state's diversity; the governor became eligible for reelection; the numerous and diverse boards and commissions were reduced to twenty-two in number and placed directly under the governor and cabinet; and staff size was expanded to help manage state government more effectively.

During this same period, the state framework for creating and managing local governments was also modernized. Much like state government, local government authority was distributed to a number of separately elected "constitutional officers," including a sheriff, property appraiser, clerk of the courts, supervisor of elections, and tax collector. The new Constitution of 1968, along with the statutory initiatives of the 1970s, gave citizens in each county the authority to restructure their county government as they saw fit.

Despite these important reforms, Florida continued to have the most fragmented government of any state in the nation. At the state level, Florida remains the only state to invest executive authority in a governor and cabinet system, with six separately elected cabinet officials. At the local level, citizens have achieved little success in dismantling the fiefdoms of local constitutional officers.

Reform efforts since the mid-1970s have been aimed at bringing further cohesion to state and local government and addressing the massive population expansion. But such efforts continue to be frustrated. The governor and other state and local leaders have sought to facilitate comprehensive planning at the state, regional, and local levels through legislative and constitutional initiatives (see chapter 4 for a more detailed discussion of growth management). Suffice it to say that the state legislature and the other cabinet officers have repeatedly blocked efforts to strengthen the hand of the governor in this process.

### The Legislative Branch

"Hide the women, children, and pets, the Florida legislature is back in session," went the old adage whenever Florida's political leaders convened in Tallahassee. During the days of "pork chop" dominance in the 1950s, Floridians had little confidence in the state legislature. Too many things could happen when the porkchoppers assembled, and most of them were bad from the point of view of residents of south Florida.

Despite actions to modernize the state legislature in the 1968 Constitution and in the Legislative Reorganization Act of 1969, the legislature still conjures up voter concern whenever it convenes. Few Floridians believe the legislature has much vision; indeed, most seem convinced that its leaders are primarily concerned with obtaining special programs for their districts. The legislature's reputation suffers in part because of the fragmentation in its authority through the historic practice of rotating legislative leaders every two years. In the U.S. Congress and in many state legislatures, the speaker of the House and president of the

Senate can maintain their positions indefinitely. A longer tenure in office enables these leaders to become more proficient at their positions and knowledgeable about the needs of their constituencies. Because it also allows these individuals to accrue substantial power, which some may take advantage of, it enhances decision making and accountability. In Florida, however, power remains diffused, rotating among various leaders and special-interest groups within the legislature. It is a system not designed to promote leadership and accountability. Instead, legislative leaders are often more interested in delivering benefits to their hometowns because their tenure at the top is so brief.

Florida's bicameral legislature faced further fragmentation with the 1992 adoption of the so-called Eight Is Enough amendment to the Constitution, which limits state senators and representatives to no more than eight consecutive years of service. Members of the House of Representatives currently serve two-year terms and will be limited to four terms under the 1992 amendment, and senators currently serve four-year terms and will be limited to two consecutive terms. Senators and representatives are elected from single-member districts apportioned on the basis of population, so that each senator and each representative represents roughly the same number of people. To maintain the balance among districts, the legislature is reapportioned every ten years, upon completion of the Federal Census.

Although the House and the Senate are virtually equal in their powers, they differ in two respects. First, the House and Senate exercise different roles in the process of removing a governor from office. The House votes on articles of impeachment, while the Senate is the body in which an impeached governor is tried. Impeachment does not mean that the governor is removed from office, only that he or she is to be tried by the Senate. This is the same process followed by the federal government in removing a president.

The second difference between the House and the Senate is that the latter confirms executive appointments. The Senate's role in confirming appointments has proven to be rather important, especially since Republicans took control of the Senate in the 1990s. For example, the Senate refused to confirm the nomination of Jim Towey to serve as secretary for children and family services in 1996 because he was a close political ally of Chiles. To embarrass him politically and to show the governor that they have their own political weapons to limit his authority, senators have also held up some of Chiles's other appointments.

Both the House and the Senate must concur for legislation to be enacted, and bills may originate in either house. These procedures differ slightly from those in the U.S. Congress, particularly in the case of appropriations bills, which on the national level must originate in the House of Representatives.

Like most complex organizations, the Florida legislature has a specialized language for describing its activities and projects. A proposal to be considered by the legislature is referred to as a bill. If the bill is passed by both houses and approved by the governor or allowed by the governor to become law without his or her signature (or if the governor's veto is overridden), the bill becomes a law. After the law has been incorporated into the state's body of laws, it becomes a statute.

The legislature does most of its work in committees and in legislative offices, not on the floor of the two houses. The Senate and House each have committees on education, for example, and the two committees may be further divided into subcommittees on specific subjects, such as higher education or public school education. The various committees in both houses respond to bills assigned to them by the presiding officers of the Senate and the House. Not all committees have equal powers. In particular, the Appropriations Committee and the Rules Committee are enormously influential. The former passes on all bills authorizing the spending of money, the most important of which is the General Appropriations Bill. The Rules Committee determines when bills will be considered by the full House and Senate and also has the power to revise all legislation before it goes before either body. The Finance and Tax Committee, which deals with taxes and other revenue-generating measures, also has greater significance than most of the other committees.

The most powerful legislators are the speaker of the House and the president of the Senate. Typically, legislators run for these positions internally by gathering support from their colleagues several years in advance. When a majority has been achieved for a particular year, a caucus is called so that a formal vote can be taken. If the candidate is elected at the caucus, he or she becomes known as the "Speaker Designate" or the "President Designate." However, by convention, the appointment does not become official until a special organizing session is held in November of the specified year. Usually the political party that has a majority of seats in the house controls the leadership selection process. The members of the party agree on a nominee by majority vote, and then support their nominee when the full house determines its leadership.

Coalitions between members of opposing parties have been rare in Florida politics. In 1986, Senator Dempsey Barron persuaded a group of Republicans and conservative Democrats to support his candidacy for Senate president. In 1996, Democrats endorsed Buzz Ritchie for speaker in 1997, but the fall elections left the House with a Republican majority. Ritchie's supporters tried to persuade Cuban-American members of the Republican Party in the House to vote for Ritchie in exchange for the opportunity to chair certain committees. The deal failed after much backroom negotiating, and Dan Webster, Republican from Orlando, was elected speaker.

More recently, in 1998, the Republican leadership in the House made overtures to black representatives when Democrats removed Representative Willie Logan, an African American, from his elected leadership position in the House. Republican speaker Dan Webster subsequently appointed a few black representatives to prominent legislative posts, a most unusual step in dealing with members of the other party. Webster's aim was not only to persuade black representatives that Republicans were interested in working with them, but also to reach out to their black supporters in Florida.

The power of the speaker of the House and the president of the Senate is rooted in their control of the organizational structure of their respective legislative bodies. Because they decide the committee structure of their bodies, make all committee assignments, and appoint all committee chairs, they can determine the overall course of legislation and control much of the behavior of the membership. They usually work very closely with the Appropriations chair and the chair of the

Rules Committee to further manage the legislative process. Moreover, the power of the speaker and Senate president is augmented by their ability to hire and fire all legislative staff and control all staff assignments to committees.

Political influence in the Florida legislature often has little to do with seniority. More important are connections to the top leadership, especially to the speaker of the House and the president of the Senate, and knowledge of the legislative process. Because of his mastery of parliamentary procedures, W. D. Childers, senator from Pensacola since 1970, has been one of the most influential members of the Senate despite representing one of the most sparsely settled areas of the state. Childers knows how to get his bills filed, make legislative deals, and secure funding for local projects.

County delegations have also proven to be a powerful presence in the legislature and have added to the fragmentation of state politics. State senators and representatives from the same county usually meet periodically during the year, hold local hearings to seek public input, and develop a list of delegation priorities. One of the most influential delegations during the past two decades has been the one from Broward County. Members of this delegation have been very successful in securing local projects and funds for constituents and have become a model for other delegations.

In addition to individual legislators and county delegations, the House and Senate staff are powerful in their own right. They handle the details of legislation, manage the flow of legislation from bill drafting to final passage, and provide continuity from one session to the next. Many staffers, especially those involved in the budget process, accumulate substantial influence by virtue of their expertise. Senators and representatives cannot function effectively without them. Historically, the Senate staff has been more removed from partisan politics than the House staff. Staff for the latter body is often assigned to individual members and follows them from committee to committee as their assignments change from year to year. Inevitably, this pulls them into political allegiances. By contrast, Senate staffers are assigned to committees and usually do not move when the committee membership changes. The consequence is that, when the House leadership changes, as it did in 1997, the House staff is much more prone to turnover than the Senate.

One of the most important responsibilities of the legislature is to produce an annual budget. The Florida Constitution, like those in most other states, explicitly prohibits deficit spending. To assist the legislature and governor in developing an annual budget, analysts from both the legislature and governor's office provide estimates of revenue on a quarterly basis. Beginning in June, the governor's office and executive agencies begin preparing their budget requests for the next legislative session in light of the revenue forecast. In the fall of each year, the Appropriations Committees develop their separate budgets. Since the two bills usually differ, the president of the Senate and the speaker of the House appoint a conference committee to produce a single compromise bill, which is then sent back to both houses for a vote. This bill cannot be amended; legislators can only vote for or against the conference committee's budget.

Legislative dominance of the budget process has helped to further undermine unity in state government. The governor's office exerts only modest influence in assembling the budget, because the legislature prepares the budget independent of the governor's recommendations. In fact, when the governor's office receives budget requests from the executive agencies so that it can prepare an executive budget for legislative consideration, these same requests must also (by law) be sent directly to the House and Senate, because the two houses assemble their appropriation bills before the governor's recommendations arrive. Adding to the lack of coherence in the budget preparation process, the speaker and Senate president seldom exert much control over the process, other than identifying policy priorities and a few personal "turkeys" for their home communities. The appropriations process generally takes place from the bottom up, which means that it is often chaotic and unpredictable.

The Florida Constitution provides the governor with a line-item veto, which allows him to cut any single budget item that the legislature has funded. The legislature can override the governor's veto, but only by a two-thirds vote in both chambers of the legislature. Governors can make an override difficult for legislators by vetoing a measure after the session has adjourned, thus preventing legislators from reconsidering the measure until the legislature reconvenes in the following year or in special session. Nevertheless, the governor's veto is at best a defensive weapon. It can be used to defeat measures, but it cannot build support. And it has little value in setting the legislative agenda or in bringing order to Florida's legislative process.

The legislature meets for sixty days beginning on the first Tuesday after the first Monday in March. The date had been changed from April to March in response to concerns from legislators that under the previous calendar too much business was being done in the last week of the session, and in the rush to get out of Tallahassee, legislators who had planned family vacations or made business commitments in June quickly approved last-minute proposals without adequate study. Legislative sessions may be extended by a three-fifths vote of each house. The legislature may also meet in special session when the governor or the presiding officers acting jointly decide to consider particular topics.

## The Executive Branch

A governor, lieutenant governor, and a cabinet of six officers who are elected by statewide vote are collegially responsible for Florida's executive branch. The governor and lieutenant governor run for office on a single ticket and can serve for a maximum of two consecutive terms of four years each. The cabinet officers are also limited to two four-year terms by the eight-year term limit established for most elected state offices in 1992.

Even more so than the legislative branch, the single defining characteristic of Florida's executive branch is fragmentation, which has been created by requiring the governor to share power with the state cabinet. This situation has persisted in Florida since the nineteenth century. The 1968 Constitution states that the governor has "supreme executive power," but in reality the governor is merely the first among equals.

The presence of elected officials in the executive branch in addition to the governor was provided for in the 1885 Constitution as a way to limit the authority of the governor. The establishment of a cabinet was very common in American states during the late nineteenth century, and it has remained prominent in several states today. What has made the Florida cabinet different, however, is the manner in which these seven officials have operated. During the late nineteenth and twentieth centuries, the Florida cabinet met on a regular, typically weekly, basis. Through custom as well as statute, the governor has chaired the meetings, but he had no other special privileges. His voice and vote are simply one among seven.

In the 1885 Constitution, Sections 21 through 27 of Article IV defined the duties of each cabinet official and granted to each "such other duties as shall be prescribed by law." This clause gave rise to many anomalies over time, which served to fragment the executive branch further and undermine the authority of the governor. In particular, as boards and commissions were created to address state needs in a particular period, they were occasionally assigned to one of the cabinet officials instead of the governor. Inevitably, the creation of numerous agencies over time and their assignment to members of the cabinet undermined the authority and power of the governor.

Governors were not, however, completely without resources to overcome the political fragmentation of the executive branch. Alliances with cabinet members, even on an ad hoc basis, helped further gubernatorial initiatives. Patronage also strengthened the governor's hand. While individual cabinet members had patronage of their own, the governor had many more appointments available to him, which he could use to enhance ties with certain cabinet officials.

During the late nineteenth century and the first two-thirds of the twentieth century, the governor and the cabinet officials were all Democrats, suggesting that alliances would be relatively easy to form. But the dominance of the Democratic Party in this era created a party in which individual allegiances were typically more important than party ties. Moreover, some of these very cabinet officials had their eyes on the governor's office and were not necessarily inclined to help the current governor succeed. Then there were cabinet officials who served for more years than the governor had been an adult, and these men often believed they had a better understanding of state needs than the governor did. Nathan Mayo, for example, served as commissioner of agriculture with nine different governors over a thirty-seven-year period;

R. A. Gray was secretary of state for thirty years; and Doyle Connor was commissioner of agriculture for thirty years. These three men developed extensive political connections with legislative leaders and had little need for the governor's patronage. Moreover, they brooked little interference from the governor's office in their areas of responsibility.

Many governors have had public disagreements with cabinet members, which only served to splinter executive leadership further. Both Spessard Holland and Millard Caldwell often disagreed with their irascible attorney general, Tom Watson. On one particular occasion, during an intense cabinet meeting, Watson invited Governor Holland "to settle the dispute outside by more direct means than just a debate." Eventually others intervened to calm him down. On another occasion, the cabinet under Governor LeRoy Collins approved the expenditure of $300,000 for repairs to the state capitol building while Collins was on a trip to Washington, D.C. Collins had previously expressed his opposition to the expenditure, but his colleagues decided to go ahead without him.

Throughout this period, governors came and went, but cabinet officers, like Tom Watson, often stayed. Between 1885 and 1959 only four cabinet officials who were seeking reelection suffered defeat. From 1901 to 1970, discounting two brief temporary cabinet appointments, the members of the cabinet served an average of nearly twelve years in office. Meanwhile, the governor served his single four-year term and returned home, no longer a force in state politics, except in the rare circumstance when he was elected to the U.S. Senate, and that has occurred on only three occasions in the twentieth century, with the elections of Park Trammell, Spessard Holland, and Bob Graham. Lawton Chiles did it in reverse, serving first in the Senate and then as governor.

Although the governor had little influence over certain parts of the executive branch, including a number of agencies and boards, the public has held "him accountable . . . for the complete operation of the executive branch." This remains equally true today. A poll taken in 1997, for example, revealed that Floridians had general praise for the governor when political and economic conditions in the state were good, but denounced him when they felt conditions had deteriorated.

Moreover, when insurance companies responded slowly to needs of Floridians in the wake of a Hurricane Andrew, the citizens criticized the governor, not the insurance commissioner. And so it goes from schools to agriculture to the prosecution of murderers and felons. The Constitution might well have empowered the cabinet to serve as the executive branch on these issues, but the public looked to the governor to lead the state and protect its citizens.

To prevent the executive branch from working at cross purposes and thereby forcing a complete breakdown in government operations under the 1885 Constitution, ex officio boards were established to provide for a certain unity of policy and procedure. Some of these boards have been exceedingly important in the development of public policy. The Budget Commission, for example, drew up a biennial budget that often shaped state policy from the late nineteenth century up to 1970. Originally there were twenty-two boards or commissions, and the number increased steadily over the years until it reached over 200 in 1968. During World War II, the number had grown to thirty, and the governor sat on nineteen separate boards, while the secretary of state sat on ten, the comptroller on thirteen, the treasurer on seventeen, and the attorney general on seventeen. During the war years, the responsibilities on each of these officials was enormous, and they were only complicated further by the numerous boards and commissions on which they also served. The constitutional-structural arrangements diffused and decentralized administrative authority at a time when they should have been centralized so that the state could respond promptly to the wartime crises it faced. Such was not the case in Florida.

When the Florida Constitution was rewritten in 1968, an effort was made to bring order and cohesion to the executive branch. Today's cabinet officers perform two main functions. First, each one oversees a department, which handles functions associated with the cabinet official's specialty. For example, the commissioner of education administers policies for the public education system throughout the state. Similarly, the attorney general oversees the Department of Legal Affairs, which represents the state in legal disputes.

Secondly, the cabinet officers sit collegially with the governor on a number of boards. Some of these boards exist as a last court of appeal for disputes between local governments, executive agencies, private citizens, and other parties. Others make policy for some of the subjects handled by individual cabinet officers. For example, the governor and cabinet sit as the State Board of Education, which sets policy for the commissioner of education. The governor and cabinet also oversee four departments. These are the Department of Law Enforcement, the Department of Highway Safety and Motor Vehicles, the Department of Revenue, and the Department of Veterans Affairs.

Because the governor and the cabinet are confronted with a wide array of issues, most of their collective decisions are perfunctory. They generally endorse the recommendations of staff members who have deliberated "out of the sunshine." Issues that capture public attention, however, do gain the attention of the full cabinet and are often deliberated at meetings in which the governor and cabinet function like a county or city commission responding to angry constituents. Land acquisition by the state and environmental policies are those most likely to generate public outcry.

Efforts to reform the cabinet system have achieved very little success. In 1995, the Citizens Commission on Cabinet Reform was appointed by Governor Chiles, the cabinet officers, the speaker of the House, and the president of the Senate. Its chair was former governor Reubin Askew, a Democrat, and its vice-chair was former governor Bob Martinez, a Republican. After reviewing over 400 statutes that assigned collegial responsibilities to the governor and the cabinet, the commission recommended unanimously that many of these responsibilities be assigned directly to the governor or to one of the cabinet officers. Even with a unanimous vote by commission members and the support of executive and legislative leaders, the commission's recommendations were rejected by the legislature, with the sole exception of those that applied to education.

Despite this defeat, as the new century dawns cabinet reform appears to have a greater chance at success than at any previous time in Florida history, because of term limits and bipartisan support for reform among party leaders. Cabinet members are now prohibited from serving more than eight consecutive years, and Senate and House members are limited to eight consecutive years. Because leaders in the two chambers and in the cabinet frequently aspire to be governor, they now face the fairly immediate prospect that limits on that office will constrain their own ability to function effectively as governor.

In the face of a fragmented executive branch, the governor must use all his powers to elevate his voice and authority above the other cabinet officers. As previously noted, the governor can sponsor and veto legislation, and he has the power to veto line items in the General Appropriations Act. The Florida governor also appoints the heads of a number of agencies, including the Departments of Transportation, Commerce, Community Affairs, Business and Professional Regulation, Health, Children and Family Services, Environmental Protection, Citrus, Corrections, Juvenile Justice, Labor and Employment Security, Lottery, Elder Affairs, and Management Services. The agency heads often meet together in a group known informally as "the Little Cabinet." Because they are appointed by the governor and dependent on him for their positions, they work closely with him to carry out his agenda.

A third power conferred upon the governor is the authority to make appointments to almost a thousand boards. Some of these boards are extremely important and highly visible. For example, the governor appoints all members to the state Board of Regents, which governs the State University System, and to Florida's Water Management Districts, which levy taxes and implement programs to maintain drainage projects and protect the state's water supply. Other boards are smaller but nevertheless important. These include hospital boards, the boards of community colleges, regional planning councils, and hundreds of local boards. The governor also fills elected offices at the state and local levels that have been vacated in midterm, with the exception of members of the state legislature. The governor has the power to appoint replacements for U.S. senators, cabinet officers, and local government officials who for one reason or another do not complete their full terms. (Special elections are required for filling vacancies in the U.S. House of Representatives.)

The governor's authority to appoint members to boards and commissions can be an effective tool for rewarding supporters and punishing opponents, and thus can be used to build and maintain political power at the grassroots level. Governor Chiles demonstrated how this appointment authority can be wielded in Broward County in the 1990s. Hamilton Forman, a prominent landowner, philanthropist, and political activist, served for many years on the board of the North Broward Hospital District. In 1990, Forman made the mistake of supporting incumbent governor Bob Martinez against Chiles in the 1990 gubernatorial campaign. Chiles, who is well known for having a "long memory," refused to reappoint Forman when his term expired, selecting instead a local, loyal Democrat. Board appointments are not particularly visible, but they are very significant in building and maintaining support in communities throughout the state.

Lastly, the governor has perhaps his most important power—the power of persuasion. More than any other official in state government, including the cabinet officers as well as the speaker of the House and the president of the Senate, the governor is perceived as the spokesperson for the interests of the state as a whole. This role gives the governor considerable influence in shaping public opinion. Citizens look to the governor to help solve most state problems, from hurricane destruction to crime and violence, roads, health care, and public education. In the 1990s, Governor Lawton Chiles successfully lobbied citizens to support the state's lawsuit against the tobacco industry after legislators threatened to stop it. This position of leadership, of course, can be a double-edged sword in that the public often holds the governor accountable for problems and conditions over which he may have little control.

## The Judicial Branch

In contrast to the executive and legislative branches of government in Florida, the court system functions in a cohesive manner. The 1972 revision of Article V of the 1968 Constitution facilitated this process by creating four levels of courts in Florida—the Supreme Court, District Courts of Appeal, Circuit Courts, and County Courts. The first two are known as appellate courts, while the latter two are trial courts. Minor courts such as justices of the peace courts, municipal courts, traffic courts, and other special courts, which had become lucrative sources of patronage for political leaders in Florida, were done away with in 1975. This new court system was supposed to be funded entirely by the state to ensure that local political interference did not affect its integrity. In reality, however, the state legislature has shifted more and more financial responsibility for the courts to the county commissions. Today, about half of the cost of the courts is provided by the counties, threatening their political independence.

The Florida Supreme Court stands at the top of the court system in Florida and reviews lower court decisions to ensure conformity with Florida law, the Florida Constitution, and the U.S. Constitution. The chief justice presides over a panel that includes six associate judges. Each justice is elected to a term of six years, and the position of chief justice is rotated among the members in two-year cycles. The chief justice is normally the senior member of the court who has not already served as chief justice, but exceptions do occur if the designated justice is not interested or because of personal disability or scandal. The court decides all cases with a minimum quorum of five justices, but at least four must concur for a decision to be reached. Tradition and constitutional rulings require the court to hear appeals from all trial courts where the death penalty has been imposed and to review decisions of district court rulings that strike down state laws or parts of the State Constitution, or decisions of one district court that are in conflict with another. The Supreme Court also has authority to review, at its discretion, a variety of decisions by the District Courts. At the request of the governor, the Florida Supreme Court can issue advisory opinions on the governor's constitutional responsibilities. The decisions of the State Supreme Court are final and can be appealed only to the U.S. Supreme Court in matters involving the federal Constitution.

The District Courts of Appeal comprise the second tier of courts in the state judicial system. The legislature has divided the state into five appellate court districts. The main function of District Courts is to hear appeals from trial courts in their geographical areas. The First District Court of Appeals also hears appeals from all over the state in those matters involving state agencies. Panels consisting of three judges hear appeals, and two judges must concur for a decision to be reached. The number of judges on any one district court varies depending upon workload.

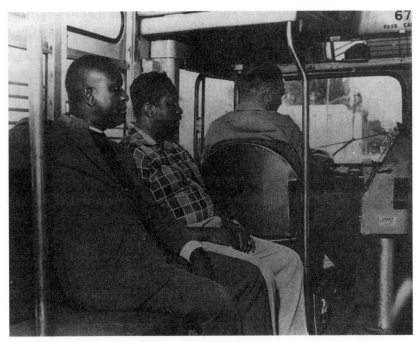

After successful bus boycotts in Montgomery, Alabama, and Tallahassee, Florida, the Miami NAACP sought legal avenues to desegregate the transit system in Miami. Here the Reverend Theodore Gibson of the Miami NAACP sat at the front of the bus to test the court-ordered desegregation of the bus lines, which occurred in 1957. (Historical Association of Southern Florida, Miami)

Governor Farris Bryant and his wife, Julia, met supporters for breakfast on the morning of his inauguration, January 3, 1961. Bryant was one of the first governors to use television extensively in his campaign to reach Florida's large and widely scattered population. He confronted widespread civil rights activism during his term of office. (Florida State Archives)

Civil rights issues dominated Florida politics in the 1950s and 1960s, and demonstrations in St. Augustine in 1964 assumed particular prominence when the Reverend Martin Luther King, Jr., and the Southern Christian Leadership Conference joined forces with local activists to desegregate what King called "the oldest segregated community in America." Here police officer Henry Billitz, in plain clothes, dove into the pool at Monson's Motor Lodge in St. Augustine to arrest those participating in a civil rights demonstration. (Associated Press Wirephoto Service)

The Southern Christian Leadership Conference and its supporters sought to show the nation the extremes of segregation in the South, where even the ocean beach had sections for blacks and whites. Here police chased and beat civil rights demonstrators along St. Augustine Beach and pursued them into the Atlantic Ocean. (Associated Press Wirephoto Service)

The arrest of Mrs. Malcolm Peabody (*seated left*), mother of Governor Endicott Peabody of Massachusetts, signaled the beginning of the Southern Christian Leadership Conference's national campaign in St. Augustine. Events there hurt the reputation of the community and the state for moderation and set back tourism several years. (From the files of the *St. Augustine Record*)

The Reverend Martin Luther King, Jr., accompanied children picketing in St. Augustine in 1964 against segregation. Governor Farris Bryant proved unable to guide the state through this crisis in the peaceful manner of LeRoy Collins during the crisis over school desegregation in the 1950s. (Associated Press Wirephoto Service)

Marjory Stoneman Douglas (*left*) and Marjorie Carr (*right*) championed efforts to save Florida's environment. In her book *The Everglades: River of Grass*, Douglas spoke eloquently about Florida's last frontier; Carr founded the Florida Defenders of the Environment and blocked construction of the Cross-Florida Barge Canal which threatened the freshwater aquifer and Florida's scenic and sensitive Ocklawaha River. (Carr's photo by David Godfrey; Florida State Archives)

Mrs. Alfred I. (Jessie) duPont with her brother, Ed Ball, who managed the giant politically influential duPont conglomerate. From the 1930s to his death in 1981, Ball exercised extraordinary economic and political influence in Florida. Few politicians dared challenge him, and even fewer continued in office when they did. (Florida State Archives)

Governor Claude Kirk giving his state-of-the-state message to the Democratic-controlled legislature. He was constantly at odds with legislators over his agenda and over his public posturing when they failed to pass his programs. (P. K. Yonge Library of Florida History)

Claude Kirk relished the limelight. Here he appeared with the mysterious "Madame X," as he called her, who subsequently became Mrs. Kirk. His controversial and often outlandish behavior ultimately alienated voters and set the Republican Party back for a generation. (Florida State Archives)

Governor Claude Kirk met with Republican Vice Presidential candidate Spiro Agnew in Jacksonville in 1968. Florida was an important state for Agnew and Republican presidential candidate Richard Nixon as they sought to capture the White House in 1968. Florida voted for them, but both were subsequently forced to resign before the ends of their terms because of scandals. (Florida State Archives)

Governor Claude Kirk met with Florida A&M's legendary football coach Jack Gaither and spoke to the players. Kirk's position on racial advancement confused Floridians: He seemed to have no personal racial prejudice and supported an end to racial violence, but politically he often took a stance that was at odds with his personal philosophy but that would, he thought, help him politically. In 1970 he seized control of the public schools in Manatee County to prevent busing to facilitate integration. He was subsequently held in contempt by the federal courts, and he damaged race relations in the state in the process. (Florida State Archives)

Six of Florida's postwar governors posing together: (*left to right*) C. Farris Bryant, LeRoy Collins, Charley E. Johns, Reubin O'D. Askew, Millard F. Caldwell, and W. Haydon Burns. Florida's traditionally "weak" governor produced, nevertheless, two of the most prominent governors in the nation in the twentieth century— Collins and Askew. (Florida State Archives)

Florida's economic development and international reputation were spurred by the development of the Cape Canaveral space facility in the 1960s. No event stirred more attention than the launch of Apollo XI on July 16, 1969, with astronauts Neil A. Armstrong, Michael Collins, and Edwin E. Aldrin (*left to right*). Armstrong and Aldrin were the first to walk on the moon. (Florida State Archives)

Despite pressures from black citizens and supportive whites, race relations were slow to improve in Florida. Here Joseph W. Hatchett of Pinellas County posed with his family as he became Florida's first African-American Supreme Court justice in 1975. He served for four years and resigned to accept an appointment to the Federal Court of Appeals. (Florida State Archives)

Below the appellate courts stand the trial courts, which constitute the last two tiers of Florida's four-tier judicial system. Circuit Courts represent the third tier and are located in certain designated geographical areas as established by the state legislature. In 1996, Florida had twenty circuits, with each Circuit Court presided over by a circuit judge, who is elected for a term of six years. Circuit Courts handle felony trials in which offenses are punishable by imprisonment in the state corrections system (usually for a term of at least one year). Circuit Courts also hear appeals from county courts and from local government code enforcement boards.

The fourth tier comprises the county courts. Each county has a county court and one or more judges. These courts handle small civil cases, most misdemeanors, and all alleged violations of municipal and county ordinances. The county judges serve for four years and are elected by countywide vote.

Through a special process, the governor fills all judicial vacancies. A Judicial Nominating Committee reviews prospective candidates and presents the governor with a list of three qualified nominees, from which the governor selects one. The Judicial Nominating Committee is made up of three members selected by the Board of Governors of the Florida Bar, three members appointed by the governor, and three members selected by the other six members of the committee.

Judicial elections differ for appellant and trial courts. In the case of appellant courts, after the governor fills a vacancy, the judge serves for at least one year, and then his or her record is submitted to the voters to see if the judge should be retained in office. If the incumbent does not receive a majority of the votes cast, the process begins again with the Judicial Nominating Commission screening potential candidates.

By contrast, trial courts do not have these merit retention elections. An effort to provide a merit retention system for trial judges has been rejected by voters on two separate occasions. County and district judges serve for terms of four years and are subject to nonpartisan, competitive elections. These elections place trial court judges in the awkward position of accepting campaign contributions from attorneys, many of whom subsequently appear before the court representing a variety of clients. It is a system that inevitably undermines the integrity of the courts and the judges.

The reform act of 1972 eliminated the justices of the peace, in large measure because they were perceived as patronage positions that ill served the court system. But, in the twenty years since then, many, including the current chief justice Gerald Kogan, believe that neighborhood courts may be central to ensure civil behavior in local areas. Kogan and others contend that such courts are close to the people and bring considerable social pressure on local residents to act in a civil manner because their illegal behavior will become known to their friends and neighbors. The Supreme Court is currently experimenting with a neighborhood court system in Tallahassee to determine its effectiveness in settling local disputes and in improving civil behavior.

## Other Levels of Government

The fragmentation of state government in Florida is exacerbated by federal programs and by local governments. All state governments are vested in the U.S. Constitution and cannot be disestablished by constitutional amendment. By contrast, local governments—except Dade and Duval counties, both of which have powers vested in the Florida Constitution—are creatures of state law and can be created, abolished, or altered simply by a majority vote of the legislature. One might expect that these arrangements would enhance state control, but this has not been the case. Instead, the state finds its responsibilities and authority frequently whipsawed by the numerous governments, agencies, and federal programs that impinge upon it.

### FEDERAL GOVERNMENT

The Federal Government has limited authority over state governments because the U.S. Constitution specifically restricts its powers to those enumerated in the Constitution and reserves all other powers to the states and the people. In the words of the Tenth Amendment, "The powers not delegated to the United States by the Constitution, nor prohibited by it to the states, are reserved to the states respectively, or to the people." State governments may design their own constitutions, maintain a state militia, establish their own legal codes and judicial systems, and take responsibility for a host of public services and facilities ranging from transportation to education.

The State of Florida and the federal government interact in three significant areas. First, as with other states in the union, Florida is heavily dependent upon the federal government for social insurance programs, particularly Medicaid, which provides health insurance to the poor. The federal government will match approximately dollar for dollar the amount provided by the state for health care to persons meeting criteria established in federal legislation. Medicaid is particularly important to Florida because much of it covers nursing home care for the elderly. With more than 18 percent of the population over sixty-five years of age in 1998, Florida is heavily dependent on Medicaid funding to care for the needs of its elderly population, and any changes in Medicaid funding and related programs have far-reaching implications for the state.

A second area where federal policy affects Florida more than it does in most states is in the area of immigration. During the past four decades, Florida has been a magnet for refugees from other countries, especially Central America and the Caribbean. These immigrants have contributed extensively to the state's diversity and economic vibrancy, but they have also burdened state and local government. Many have needed special services to help them and their children adjust to their new society, find employment, and attend school. In large part this financial responsibility resides with the states, not with the federal government. Federal policy is therefore crucial to Florida as it seeks to address the needs of its immigrant population. Despite similar experiences in California, Texas, and New Mexico, representatives from these states have been unsuccessful in persuading their colleagues from the other states to provide federal assistance to offset the costs of legal and illegal immigration.

Federal initiatives in defense and space have constituted a third area of vital interest to the state. Florida's economic development was revitalized during World War II by the construction of Air Force and Naval bases. Two decades later, Florida became the launching pad for space exploration because of its southern geographical location and its good weather. The enormous federal investment in the Kennedy Space Center has brought many skilled and high-paying jobs and advanced technology industries to Florida. Any diminishing of that investment, as occurred in the 1990s, has a significant effect on the state's economy.

LOCAL GOVERNMENT

Beneath state government are local governments, of which Florida has three kinds. The local governments with which citizens are most familiar are cities and counties. State law creates both, but they have somewhat different functions, at least in theory. Florida has sixty-seven counties, all of which were created prior to 1940. Counties are intended to carry out state responsibilities at a local level. These responsibilities are the same for all counties except for those that adopt a local charter and revise their structure. Every county has a county commission and a set of constitutional officers, such as a sheriff, a property appraiser, and a supervisor of elections.

In contrast, cities are tailored to address the needs and concerns of specific communities. Their political structure also varies substantially, depending on local preferences. Florida currently has 401 cities, most of which have professional city managers that run the municipal bureaucracy and report to a city council that sets policy. A few cities have an elected mayor who manages the city bureaucracy. There are also other variations that combine different aspects of the city manager and strong mayor forms of municipal government.

Both cities and counties vary greatly in population. Many of the counties are quite rural; thirty of the sixty-seven have populations under 50,000. A handful are highly urbanized. Dade County is the most urbanized, with over 2 million residents, while Broward has over 1.3 million. Similarly, Florida's cities range in size from Jacksonville, with 718,000 people and a unified city-county government, to Miami, with 365,000, to Orchard, with twenty-five, and Islandia, with thirteen.

Local government in Florida remains even more fragmented than state government. Florida has no set pattern in its city-county relations. In some counties, many services are delivered by one or more cities, and the county government has few urban service responsibilities. Tallahassee and Leon County, and Pensacola and Escambia County are examples of this sort of relationship. In other areas of the state there are only a few cities, and the county operates like a large city. This is explicitly the case with Duval County, which combined Jacksonville and the other local governments in the county in 1967, and it is also true to a lesser extent of Hillsborough County, in which Tampa is located. In other instances, such as in Dade, Broward, Palm Beach, and Orange counties, the cities encompass much of their respective counties, and city and county governments compete with each other for consumers. Lastly, many sections of Florida have small populations, and they have rural county governments and small municipalities.

The third form of local government is the special-purpose district. Special districts differ from cities and counties in that their responsibilities are narrowly focused on one or two areas. Like many other states, Florida has special districts for hospital care, water management, fire protection, and drainage. Some districts cover more than one county, while some are coterminous with county borders and some are geographically smaller than counties and cities. A few special districts have taxing authority, but most do not. Special districts are usually established by acts of the legislature, and such legislation usually specifies how the districts' boards of directors are to be appointed. Officials for some districts are appointed by the governor, while for other districts they are elected, are local appointees, or are chosen by a combination of methods.

Because of its rapid population growth, Florida has experienced difficulty in matching local forms of government to urban needs. Large areas of many counties are thoroughly urbanized, and yet municipal governments do not serve them. This leaves county governments, which are designed principally to oversee large rural areas, trying to deliver city-like services. To some extent the gap between county and municipal structures is filled by special districts, but the large number of districts now in place creates other problems for local residents.

The largest special districts in Florida are the water management districts, each of which covers several counties. The South Florida Water Management District, for example, extends from Orange County in central Florida to Key West and includes all or parts of seventeen counties. These districts originated to provide flood protection but have gradually evolved into operations that have broad water resource and management responsibilities. The boards of the water management districts are also lucrative sources of patronage for the governor, although the Senate must confirm board members. The districts are funded by property taxes.

While school districts are not designated as special districts under the Florida Constitution, they function as such for all practical purposes. Their boundaries are coterminous with counties, and they are funded by a combination of state general revenues, utility taxes, and local property taxes. The geographic size of Florida's school districts facilitated the school desegregation process in the state in the late 1960s and 1970s, but they have also been characterized of late as excessively large and unwieldy bureaucracies. The school districts of Broward and Orange counties have been criticized heavily in the press for being extravagant in their spending, constructing large "palaces" to house their administrative offices, and being insular in their thinking.

In an effort to bring order and efficiency to local government, the 1968 Constitution gave voters control over county government. A majority of voters are free to adopt a "home-rule charter," which is like a local constitution. As of 1997, sixteen counties had adopted home-rule charters. While few counties have been successful in using this approach to eliminate constitutional officers, many have used it to deal with specific issues. Several have moved from countywide elections of county commissioners to elections within subcounty single-member districts. Others have established countywide planning councils to oversee land use regulation. Transportation has also been singled out on occasion by charter counties for countywide financing and planning.

Political struggles over county charters offer some of the most interesting spectacles in Florida politics. Palm Beach County is one example where initial attempts to adopt a charter failed. In 1985, retirees and environmentalists joined forces and passed a charter that made few changes to the existing government structure. Two years later, the same coalition amended the charter to establish a countywide planning council with the authority to control zoning in cities as well as in the county. At that time Palm Beach had thirty-eight cities, the most in the state. The new countywide planning council sought to crack down on development, but city leaders rebelled and succeeded in getting voters to repeal the planning council's enabling authority. Business leaders, led by developers, then joined forces with African-American voters to change the electoral process for selecting county commissioners from at-large to single-member districts. Their purpose was to gain control of the commission by electing commissioners who resided in specific districts. The initiative was successful, but business leaders have not been able to wrest control of the commission away from supporters of limited growth. Not surprisingly, charter revision remains a hot issue in Palm Beach County.

## Local Government Fragmentation

Despite the reforms adopted under the 1968 Constitution, local government has become even more fragmented and complicated than it was prior to this period. The failure of the 1968 Constitution in this area is similar to its inability to bring cohesion to the cabinet system at the state level. The reforms produced unintended and unexpected results.

Two major factors have contributed to increasing complexity and duplication in the delivery of local government services. First, there has been tremendous growth in the unincorporated areas of Florida. This trend has resulted in a demand for services and the urbanization of county governments. Second, however, the movement of counties into urban service delivery has occurred without a commensurate reorganization of responsibilities by other service providers. As a result, counties, special districts, and cities occasionally overlap one another's services, prevent efficient service delivery by blocking economies of scale, and confront citizens with a complex, multilayered bureaucracy. In some counties, residents receive services and pay taxes and fees to the county, city, school district, water management district, hospital district, improvement district, juvenile welfare board, beach district, and a water and sewer authority. It is a Byzantine system to say the least, and one that mystifies and alienates many voters.

The state policy of supporting the delivery of urban services by county governments emerged in response to problems with the 1968 Constitution. In the early 1960s, some counties began delivering urban level services in the unincorporated areas. These services were financed by levying taxes countywide, which meant that the services in the unincorporated areas were subsidized with revenues from their cities. The 1968 Constitution sought to end this practice by prohibiting such "dual taxation" of city residents, but judicial rulings subsequently nullified the dual taxation prohibition. Consequently, the legislature enacted a law aimed at requiring counties to finance urban services with special taxes in the unincorporated areas. Specifically, the legislature authorized counties to levy an additional 10 mills in "municipal service taxing units" (MSTUs) in the unincorporated area in addition to the 10 mills counties can levy countywide. In effect, this decision by the legislature gave counties the equivalent of municipal taxing power and therefore enabled them to finance urban- or city-level public services. Many counties began to do just that. As a result, the roles of cities, counties, and special districts changed markedly in Florida in the 1970s and 1980s. In 1970 about two-thirds of the state's population resided in cities. By 1997, more than half, or over 7 million people, resided in unincorporated areas. During this period, the number of cities in Florida increased by only four, from 396 to 400. Conversely, the number of independent special districts almost doubled, so that there were more special districts in Florida than cities—the traditional providers of urban services.

Although this solved or at least mitigated the equity issue surrounding city and county taxes, it did not address the problems of service duplication and intergovernmental conflict. Delivering urban services via counties or special districts rather than cities would have worked if service responsibilities had been divided up in a rational and orderly fashion. Unfortunately, no mechanism was established for coordinating or choosing among service providers as more of them came on the scene. Instead, each area usually has developed its own set of service deliverers depending on history and happenstance. In one area, a special district might gradually expand its functions until it becomes a quasi city. In another area, services might be provided by the county and financed by MSTUs. Elsewhere, cities might have contracts to provide services to an unincorporated area, or, conversely, the county might have contracts to deliver services to various cities. In the end, overlapping services became commonplace.

In addition to the proliferation of providers of local government services, the last three decades have also witnessed an explosion in the number and complexity of programs being delivered by local governments under federal grants-in-aid. The expansion of federal grants-in-aid to local governments began under the Great Society's Economic Opportunity Act of 1964, which included programs for occupational skills training, compensatory education, higher education, and community redevelopment. Because of legitimate concerns about institutionalized racism in the South, the Economic Opportunity Act bypassed states and cities and allocated grants directly to local community action agencies (CAAs) established through the act's Community Action Program. The CAAs, which are nonprofit corporations, were intended to be the administrative mechanism for coordinating federal grants at the local level and also for mobilizing political pressure on local governments by the poor and minorities.

However, the number of federal grants quickly grew beyond the capacity of either the local CAAs or the federal agencies to manage properly. Many of the small programs funded by the Economic Opportunity Act became the nuclei for major legislative initiatives in their own right. In turn, the responsibilities of the Office of Economic Opportunity were divided up and parceled out to other federal agencies, and federal grants started being distributed to states, counties, and cities rather than to CAAs. The latter then became grantees for the state and local governments rather than central units through which coordination took place. By the early 1970s, the whole grants-in-aid system had become a vast array of disconnected programs with independent and uncoordinated channels of administration.

Further fragmentation and complexity were generated by the expansion of the welfare programs that had also been instituted during President Lyndon Johnson's administration. The welfare expansion included cash transfers under the Aid to Families with Dependent Children program, wage supplements authorized by the Supplemental Security Income program, health care services through Medicaid, and more. Because these initiatives were often extensions of programs from the New Deal era, they were implemented by an entirely different set of agencies, separate from both the CAAs and the local governments. In the end, very little fit together. Different federal programs provided different benefits, had different eligibility criteria, and were administered by different agencies.

Florida's local governments now face mounting pressures. They must simultaneously meet the needs of a rapidly urbanizing population while managing federal and state reductions in welfare and in federal grants-in-aid. Unfortunately, local politics usually stand in the way of much-needed reform. The result can be completely irrational, as, for example, when fire departments in cities and counties refuse to respond to fires in areas immediately adjacent to them because they lack jurisdiction.

## Revising the Constitution

Standing in stark contrast to Florida's horse-and-buggy cabinet system and other atavistic remnants of the Reconstruction South is a constitutional process that provides numerous ways for citizens to amend the constitution. The designers of the 1968 Constitution wanted to ensure that the will of the majority could never be stymied again as it had in the 1950s and 1960s, when the "porkchoppers" from rural, north Florida controlled the state legislature and ignored the needs of south Florida. The 1885 Constitution offered no relief to citizens in the face of such a political situation. Citizens, for example, could not propose amendments to the 1885 Constitution.

Under the 1968 Constitution, amendments can be proposed in five ways, but they can be adopted only by voter ratification. The most common method of proposing an amendment is through the state legislature. A joint resolution containing the proposed amendment must be passed by a three-fifths vote of the membership of each house. Typically the amendment is submitted to the voters in the next general election, which occurs at least ninety days after the amendment has been endorsed by the legislature. General elections are held in November of each even-numbered year. To place a proposed amendment before the voters at a time other than the general election, each house of the legislature must call for a special election by a three-fourths vote of its members.

A second way to amend the constitution is by popular initiative. A petition describing the proposed amendment must be circulated to voters. In order for the amendment to be placed on the ballot, the petitioners must obtain signatures from at least 8 percent of the voters in at least one-half of the state's congressional districts and of the state as a whole. The 8 percent figure is based on the number of votes cast statewide and in the congressional districts in the most recent presidential election. For the statewide elections the number is normally a little under 6 million voters, which means that the petition must be signed by almost 500,000 registered voters. After sufficient signatures are gathered, the item is then placed on the ballots at the next general election. Reubin Askew first used the initiative successfully to write an ethics code into the Constitution. But since then, the process has been employed by a variety of special-interest groups in Florida. From casino gambling to taxation, these groups have brought a host of initiatives before Florida voters, seeking special favor and effectively undermining the legislature and representative democracy.

A third way to revise the constitution is through a constitutional convention. A petition calling for a convention must receive signatures from at least 15 percent of the registered voters in at least half of the congressional districts and of the state at large. As noted previously, the 15 percent figure is applied to the number of votes cast in the most recent presidential election. The final decision to hold a convention is made by the electorate. If the electorate endorses a convention, delegates to the convention are selected at the next general election. One delegate is selected from each district represented in the Florida House of Representatives. The convention is organized three weeks later in Tallahassee, and the recommendations of the convention are placed before the voters at the next general election (a little less than two years later).

The fourth way in which the Florida Constitution can be revised is through a Constitution Revision Commission. Florida is the only state in the nation that empowers an appointed commission to place constitutional changes before voters. The commission is composed of the attorney general, fifteen members selected by the governor, nine members selected by the House speaker, nine members selected by the Senate president, and three members selected by the State Supreme Court. The governor designates the chair of the commission. The Constitution Revision Commission is authorized to place any number of amendments, in any form, including an entirely new constitution, directly to the voters without going through the state legislature. The first Constitution Revision Commission authorized by the 1968 Constitution met in 1977. A new commission was organized in the spring of 1997, and will submit its proposed revisions in November 1998. The Constitution Revision Commission is slated to meet every twenty years unless the constitutional arrangements are revised through one of the four methods of constitutional reform discussed above.

Florida's periodic reexamination of the Constitution traces its intellectual roots back to Thomas Jefferson, who, during the debate over the U.S. Constitution, contended that every constitution should be subject to review and revision every twenty years by the subsequent generation. The designers of Florida's 1968 Constitution found Jefferson's argument persuasive almost 200 years later and included it as part of a systematic review of the Constitution.

The fifth way in which proposed amendments can be placed before the voters is through the Taxation and Budget Reform Commission. First established in 1990, the commission meets every ten years and can only propose measures dealing with taxation and spending.

## Constitutional Amendments since 1969

Despite the enormous potential for reforming government in Florida, there has been little or no change since 1972. Between 1968 and 1996, 105 proposed amendments were put before the Florida voters. Most of these amendments were initiated by the state legislature. The 1977 Constitution Revision Commission placed eight propositions on the ballot. All eight were rejected.

The failure of the amendments proposed by the Constitution Revision Commission in 1977 resulted from several factors. One was the large number of proposals and their complexity. Many of the amendments included multiple subjects, some of which were controversial. Second, the amendments were placed on the ballot alongside a proposal to legalize casino gambling in Florida. Reubin Askew, who was then governor, spent most of his time campaigning against the gambling proposal and gave little attention to the other amendments. Third, and perhaps most important, the commission's proposal to eliminate the elected cabinet and thereby strengthen considerably the power of the governor was considered too radical by most Floridians. The number of proposals, in combination with the effort to legalize casino gambling and to eliminate the cabinet, doomed all to defeat.

The events surrounding the cabinet proposal provide important insight into the politics of constitutional reform. Sandy D'Alemberte chaired the 1977 Constitution Revision Commission. Before the commission's work began, another commission member, Senator Dempsey Barron, a renowned political power broker and strategist, approached D'Alemberte with a request. Barron told D'Alemberte that he would be willing to support eliminating the cabinet but he wanted to make sure that D'Alemberte would side with him if he went out on such a limb. D'Alemberte, who favored the elimination of the cabinet, thought he had secured a key ally for the proposal. What D'Alemberte did not realize was that Barron sought to block any constitutional reform, and he thought a proposal to eliminate the cabinet would ensure the defeat of constitutional revision.

As the Revision Commission neared the end of its deliberations, three proposals related to the cabinet were put forth. On one extreme, some members preferred to make no changes to the cabinet at all. At the other extreme was Barron's proposal to eliminate the cabinet altogether. Former governor LeRoy Collins, who advocated eliminating just a few of the cabinet offices, staked out a position in the middle.

A vote was taken to decide between Barron's approach and the more moderate proposal by Collins. Barron's proposal was supported by exactly half the members, and the other half supported Collins' proposal. The tie had to be broken by the chair. D'Alemberte was torn, because he knew that Barron's proposal would probably be too extreme for the voters, but he had given Barron his word and fulfilled his pledge.

Constitutional amendments generally encounter broad voter support or opposition in a particular year. Often one bad item can turn the electorate against all of the items on the ballot. Figure 3 shows the number of amendments on the ballot each year. Traditionally more amendments appear on the ballot in a presidential election year than at any other time. In part this occurs because political leaders place items on the ballot in an attempt to influence turnout and thereby affect the presidential vote. In a state like Florida, which is almost evenly split between Republicans and Democrats, a small increase in turnout, especially among voters from one party or the other, can have a significant impact on the outcome of an election. Figure 4 provides a yearly breakdown of the amendments and whether they were endorsed or rejected by voters. As the figure reveals, proposed amendments are usually supported. Of the 105 amendments submitted to voters since 1969, almost eighty have been enacted.

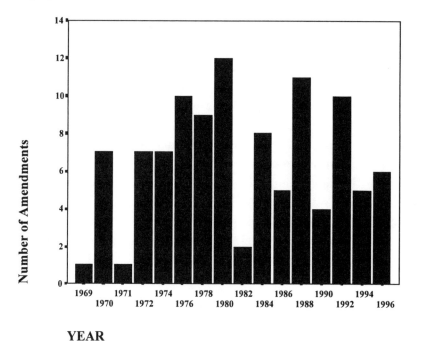

**YEAR**

Fig. 3. Total propositions presented per year.

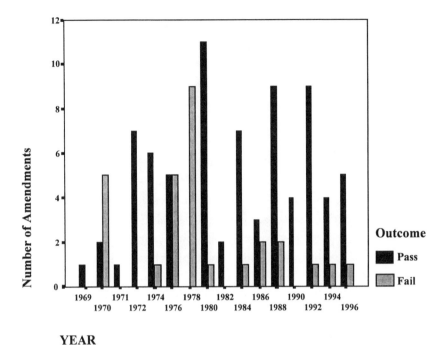

Fig. 4. Total number of amendments passing and failing, by year.

The subjects addressed by proposed amendments also make a significant difference in voter response. The most common issues are state government procedures. Other issues frequently put before the voters concern state finances, the rights of citizens, and local government finances. The highest success rate has been for state tax and finance issues. Most of these propositions placed limits on the ability of state government to tax the citizenry. The voters have been least likely to support propositions that reduce government personnel or that alter the rights of citizens.

## Conclusion

How Florida ended up with two capitol buildings is a story that reveals a great deal about the limitations on the chief executive and the fragmentation of government. Reubin Askew served as governor when the new capitol building was planned and constructed. It is still occasionally referred to as "the house that Rube built." As the plans for the new building took form, Askew proposed tearing down the old capitol or moving it to another spot. Askew envisioned the new capitol serving as a beacon for citizens. Others, including some cabinet members, urged that the old capitol be preserved and left where it was. Askew lost. The old capitol remained standing in front of the new building, the two appearing incongruous in design and size, much like Florida's government.

The constitutional limitations upon the executive branch have worked against the public interest. Two of the most important members of the state government, for example—the president of the Senate and the speaker of the House—are elected by small (substate) jurisdictions and remain in their positions for only two years. Notwithstanding a strong commitment to statewide leadership, these officers are usually preoccupied with legislative maneuvering, temporary crisis solving, and securing political benefits for their local constituents. The one political officer who might be expected to take the long view and speak for the state as a whole—the governor—can be effective only by working within this narrow political context. The consequence has been that for the last two decades Florida has lurched from crisis to crisis with many voices offering contrary solutions. One year the crisis is over transportation, the next the environment, then crime, then the budget, and then education, and then the cycle repeats itself.

Some state leaders assumed that Florida's system for budget forecasting would draw attention to emergent problems and frame some policy initiatives for the long term. But Florida budgeting, like Florida politics in general, is a game of checkers, not chess. Although studies are sometimes made of long-term trends and of the impact of such changes on the tax structure, the overriding aim of the state's budgeting system is to arrive at a consensus on the near-term budget picture. Various revenue and expenditure forecasts are made on the basis of economic activity, and the legislative and executive staffs develop a consensus estimate of the state's short-term fiscal situation.

This approach to budgeting has been very successful in depoliticizing Florida's budget forecasting process, but it has not solved the state's long-term financial picture. Public investments in education, health care, prisons, and transportation affect the state's demographic and economic composition, and therefore have a significant influence on future tax revenues. If these kinds of considerations are excluded from the budgetary process, the process tends to proceed on the assumption that current trends will prevail indefinitely. What has been lost in the process is the opportunity to make plans and positive investments in the future. Blind to the long-term implications of its policies and focusing instead on immediate budget issues, Florida's fragmented government takes the future one year at a time.

# 4 Politics, Policy, and Public Opinion

In explaining Florida politics to newcomers to the state, natives often recount an old yarn. The tale goes that a passerby sees a pig with a wooden leg in a field and stops to ask the farmer about the prosthesis. For several minutes the farmer regales the passerby with stories about the pig's many attributes. He notes that the pig fetches the newspaper in the mornings, walks the children to school, and guards the house at night. The passerby interrupts the farmer and says, "but what about the wooden leg." "Well," the farmer explains, "a pig like that you don't eat all at once."

Florida's political leaders and its citizens are a lot like the farmer. They have turned a blind eye to the implications of their actions, knowing full well that they are jeopardizing the future of their state and subsequent generations. Although Florida faces immense challenges because of its rapid population growth, antiquated government structure, aging population, fragile environment, service economy, and inadequate tax structure, the debate between Democrats and Republicans in the 1980s and 1990s has focused largely on such nonissues as who will cut the most waste and fat from government, who will build the most prisons, and who will spend state tax dollars more efficiently. Voters and political leaders blame one another for the absence of political leadership in Florida. Voters decry negative campaigning and the influence of special interests, while public officials say that, to win office, they must sidestep controversial issues and focus instead on the few basic concerns that voters share.

Both of these perspectives contain a measure of truth, but neither fully explains the limitations of state political leadership. For the past thirty years, Florida politics has revolved around a few basic issues, because the state is caught between two pressures. On the one hand, as we have seen, Florida has had to modernize politically, economically, and socially to address the needs of a dramatically expanding population—one that is increasingly ethnically and racially diverse. These developments have required state and local governments to increase spending and taxes significantly. On the other hand, this process of modernization has generated broad resistance in the state. Florida politicians have often seemed unresponsive because they are caught between the enormous needs created by massive growth and modernization and the public's unwillingness to address them adequately. What has led to this political paralysis in the state, and can anything be done to rectify it?

## Urban Sprawl

Imagine a room containing ten adult Floridians who reflect the larger adult population of the state. Seven would be from somewhere other than Florida. Of the seven, one would have resided in Florida for less than four years, and two others would have been in the state for fewer than ten years. Between 1960 and 1990, Florida's population nearly tripled, from a little under 5 million at the start of the period to over 13 million. For the better part of these three decades, the state's population has increased by an average of nearly 270,000 people per year, or an additional 743 persons every day—thirty per hour, day and night. This growth rate has slowed only slightly in the 1990s to 645 a day, and demographers predict that it will remain that way into the next century.

By the year 2000, Florida's population is projected to reach 15.5 million residents, 10 million more than in 1960.

Florida's population growth is part of a general trend throughout the Sunbelt states. For the past several decades, much of the population growth in the United States has been concentrated in Florida, Texas, and California. Between 1950 and 1990, Florida and Texas added about 10 million people, while California grew by over 17 million. Together, these three states have accounted for over 40 percent of the nation's total population growth in the past three decades.

Florida's growth has occurred in a handful of sprawling, multi-centered metropolises. Between 1970 and 1995, the bulk of Florida's population growth has occurred along the southeastern coast and in an urban corridor running across the center of the state from Tampa through Orlando to Daytona Beach. The demographic composition of the incoming population contributes to the sprawling pattern of development in the state's urban centers. Approximately one in every five persons moving into the state is over sixty-five years of age. Unlike those in other age groups, people over sixty-five can usually choose a residence without worrying about the location of their workplace. Retirees have frequently chosen to reside on the fringes of the major employment centers, notably on the outskirts of Tampa and Miami, and most recently have chosen similar areas in Charlotte, Hernando, and Collier counties. By creating their own outlying suburbs, they opt to remain close to urban amenities and yet avoid the noise, crime, taxes, and congestion of the city centers. The settlement patterns of retirees extend urban sprawl even more so than middle-class commuters who also seek a better quality of life in the suburbs but who must reside close to their workplace.

## Problems Created by Urban Sprawl

The high-growth counties in Florida have tended to follow a similar pattern of development. First, retirees move into the county, and they are followed shortly by a second wave of younger adults who provide goods and services that are required by senior citizens. A third wave of migration subsequently ensues, comprising adults who provide goods

**Table 2. Problems caused by Florida's sprawling growth**

---

Environmental
    Water pollution
    Drinking water shortages
    Destruction of wildlife and wildlife habitats
    Degradation of intact ecosystems
Social
    Urban blight
    Segregated schools
    Racial and ethnic tensions
Political
    Recurring fiscal crises
    Inadequate public facilities and services

---

and services to the second wave. As subsequent waves arrive and growth begins to affect the quality of life in the county, retirees frequently move to an adjacent county to escape the effects of urban sprawl, only to find the pattern repeating itself.

Southeast Florida has experienced this growth pattern since the 1960s. At that time, Miami Beach served as a haven for retirees. As growth enveloped the area, retirees gradually migrated to Broward County, immediately north of Miami Beach, in the 1980s. By the 1990s, retirees had begun moving north yet again to Palm Beach County, to flee urban growth, road congestion, and crime.

More recently, Florida's migration patterns on the southeast coast have been influenced by increasing arrivals of people from the Caribbean and Central America. Dade County has become the destination of choice for many immigrants from these areas. The increasing international flavor of Miami and Dade County has induced many local whites to follow senior citizens north to Broward and Palm Beach counties.

Because Florida's rapid growth and urbanization have been poorly regulated, residential and commercial development for the state's burgeoning population has generated a host of problems. These problems fall into three basic categories: environmental, social, and political (table 2). Most are caused or are exacerbated by the state's sprawling pattern of land use.

RACIAL SEGREGATION AND THE BLIGHT BELT

Florida's unregulated pattern of land development has been responsible for two intractable social problems: urban blight and racial segregation. Urban sprawl has led to urban blight and has exacerbated racial segregation in Florida because of the way the state's cities developed prior to the population explosion of the post–World War II era.

Forty years ago, when much of Florida was still agricultural farmland and the coastal towns were small, the main north-south highways–U.S. 41 on the west and U.S. 1 on the east–established informal social borders between various classes in many communities. The wealthiest residents and nearly all the urban whites lived on the coastal side of the highway, while African Americans resided farther inland. The north-south highways were the "Main Streets" around which the small towns developed. The downtowns had concentrations of shops and restaurants, motels and guestrooms for tourists, and a variety of retail shops to serve both the tourists and local residents.

The subsequent population growth and the suburbanization of Florida have had profound consequences for the old land use pattern. Because the coastal property had already been developed, expressways and malls have been built farther inland, pulling most of the shoppers and tourists from the old downtowns. Suburbs have spread inland all the way to the Everglades, leaving the old urban centers and their indigenous African-American populations behind. Today, U.S. 41 from Tampa south through Naples, and U.S. 1 from Jacksonville to Miami, weave through a belt of urban blight that extends along most of Florida's coastline. At almost any point on these roads the same pattern can be found: warehouses and deteriorating buildings, new commercial development, and gated, upscale residential areas are punctuated roughly every five miles by poor, predominantly African-American neighborhoods, most of which are adjacent to the warehouses and vacant buildings. In a few instances, such as Pearl City in Boca Raton, these minority residential areas are stable communities, but more often they are severely run down and crime ridden. Pockets of black poverty are evident in almost every older town along Florida's east and southwest coasts.

Florida's blight belt has flourished because the economy that at one time supported the state's black population has all but disappeared. Many of the agricultural jobs were lost to mechanization and urban sprawl, while microwaves, fast food, and dry cleaners replaced housekeeping and other domestic occupations. Those African Americans who were able to take advantage of the new opportunities did. But those who were too old, too young, too sick, or too lacking in education became trapped along the narrow strip of land between the old Florida and the new.

In most parts of Florida the vast majority of newcomers who arrived after World War II have been white. These new residents chose to reside in inland suburbs far from the old cities, while most African Americans were forced by economic circumstances and segregation to remain in the blight belt along the coastal highways.

During the early 1970s, school districts quickly found themselves faced with a conflict between the desire of white parents to have neighborhood schools and demands by the courts that the schools be integrated. Under pressure from federal and state judges, most of Florida's urban school districts have had to implement busing, but often they have done so in a manner that actually exacerbates the problems of the coastal areas. Because white parents have vigorously resisted having their children bused to coastal areas, school officials chose to build schools that were equidistant between the coastal cities and the inland suburbs and then bused everyone to the center. In Palm Beach County, the school board has referred to this area as the "neutral zone." In Broward County, sending black children from the same neighborhoods to central county schools in order to achieve racial balance has been coined "star bursting." The decision to bus students to this "middle ground" has minimized travel time for black and white students on the buses, but it has also led to the closing of coastal schools. The abandonment of these schools has in turn accelerated the problems facing coastal communities and further encouraged "white flight" to inland suburbs. African-American parents have also been frustrated by these educational developments, uncertain that their children have benefited by the new schools and concerned about the loss of their schools, which had constituted one of the most important institutions in the black community.

Adding to the frustration and alienation of black Floridians, state and city leaders in the 1950s and 1960s made decisions about road and neighborhood development that were racially motivated and that had devastating effects on the black community. In Miami, for example, city and state leaders ignored the concerns of black residents and deliberately built Interstate 95 so that it effectively destroyed the black community of Overtown and cordoned off the black neighborhood of Liberty City from the rest of Miami. Historian Raymond Mohl found that by the end of the era of highway construction, little remained of the Overtown that recalled its days as the Harlem of the South. The interstate construction projects, together with the massive immigration of Cubans beginning in 1959, made the needs and concerns of black Miamians invisible to the rest of the community.

## Funding Public Facilities and Services

The most serious political problem created by growth has been an endemic fiscal crisis, which has been compounded by the public's notoriously hostile attitude toward taxes. This antitax mentality in Florida is reflected by the old expression, "Don't tax you, don't tax me, tax the man behind the tree." The man behind the tree in Florida is, of course, the tourist. Public resistance to new taxes is rooted in the past, when the state was quite poor and residents barely scrapped together a living. The state's newer residents have also embraced the state's low tax structure, because they perceive that their basic needs are being met by state and local government and because they resented the high taxes they paid in their former states. J. M. "Mac" Stipanovich, a Republican activist, observed that the old saying that "what's good for General Motors is good for America" has been transformed in Florida to "What's good for me is good for Florida."

Florida's population growth, however, has placed an enormous burden on the state and local governments to provide new roads, water and sewer systems, schools, and other public services. Florida's tax structure is such that the state's leaders cannot meet this challenge without constantly going back to the voters for increases in the tax rate. Former speaker of the House T. K. Wetherell once commented that taxes were never going to get approved "until Joe Lunchbucket decides that there is a problem out there." Over the past twenty-five years, Joe and his friends have rejected the overwhelming majority of tax increases at the state and local level, as well as bond issues.

There are currently three ways in which state and local governments can raise tax revenues. They can tax property, they can tax income, and they can tax transactions or sales. Florida's tax structure is slanted heavily toward taxes on transactions. Florida is one of only seven states in the nation without an individual income tax, and its property tax is restricted by a 30 mill cap (10 mills for any single taxing unit). Florida property or ad valorem taxes are assessed on the basis of mills, with a mill being equivalent to one dollar of taxes for every $1,000 of nonexempt assessed value. A tax rate of one mill would normally generate $100 on property assessed at $100,000, but because Florida provides a homestead exemption, the first $25,000 of assessed value is excluded for year-round Florida residents. This policy has meant that a $100,000 home with a homestead exemption is taxed on only $75,000 of value and would therefore generate only $75 in ad valorem revenues for each mill. By contrast, its sales tax stands at 6 percent; only eight other states have a sales tax equal to or larger than Florida's.

The sales tax, which was first adopted in 1949, has proven to be a relatively noncontroversial source of income as well as a lucrative one, especially in a state with many part-time seasonal residents. Visitors to Florida have spent a great deal of money in the era following World War II, nearly all of which has been subject to this transaction tax. As Florida began to experience the demands of rapid growth and urban sprawl, however, it found its heavy reliance on a sales tax inadequate to meet public needs. Sales tax revenues have risen only gradually because taxable expenditures per person have remained relatively constant. Per capita revenues from a 6 percent sales tax are about $400 whether the state has 1 million or 20 million residents. By contrast, costs for urban facilities and services have increased rapidly because they are much more expensive than their rural equivalents. Wastewater treatment plants, for example, cost more than septic tanks; urban police forces with specialized units for vice and drugs cost more than road patrols;

new schools with modern facilities cost much more than older schools; and highways with overpasses and traffic signals cost more than two-lane roads with stop signs. The sales tax will remain a profitable source of revenue for Florida as long as tourism continues to expand. But, with costs rising faster than revenues, Florida has been unable through the sales tax to fund a full range of services to address the needs and problems created by its massive population growth.

## ENVIRONMENTAL DEGRADATION

Many recent arrivals to Florida find it difficult to appreciate the extent to which development has spread inland from the coast during the past fifty years. It is estimated that in the twentieth century Florida lost about half of its 20.3 million acres of wetlands. In south Florida, one way to understand the consequence of state growth is to look for cypress trees in urban areas. These trees originated in the swamps and wetlands and indicate how widespread these lands were prior to Florida's massive development. Cypress trees can still be seen in downtown Ft. Lauderdale, along the west coast of Florida, and just south of Orlando. Most of these wetlands helped preserve the state's fragile environment and its potable water. The southern region of the state, in particular, has been dependent for its water supply on underground aquifers, which are replenished by shallow surface waters flowing down the center of the state into the Everglades.

As the state's marshes and wetlands have been drained and roads constructed over them to accommodate the needs of urban residents, the environmental damage has been extensive. Florida's most serious environmental problem has been the near destruction of its natural system of water supply. As population growth has occurred in the coastal areas and as fringe areas of the Everglades have been drained and developed, the water supply in the southern part of the state has been damaged and depleted. The Everglades have been threatened further by the runoff of fertilizer and pesticides from large sugar farms to the north. Adding to the water crisis, coastal communities have experienced greater saltwater intrusion into their well fields as inland communities tap the water supply and reduce the underground flow of water toward the coast, enabling saltwater to fill the void. The result has been a shortage of potable water in the southwestern section of Florida and the emergence of "water wars," in which water-poor Pinellas County, for example, has been engaged in a heated battle with water-rich Pasco County to gain access to its water resources. Political leaders from southeast Florida have also called for piping water from the aquifers of north Florida, a region that is already none too fond of its neighbor to the south.

Water pollution in Florida has suffered as well from urbanization and the hazardous materials that have been produced by it. Dry cleaners and gas stations have posed a serious threat to Florida's environment because their wastes often contaminate the state's aquifers. Similarly, the high technology industries, which are generally but incorrectly viewed as clean industries, have also produced wastes that are dangerous to local well fields. Moreover, the pouring of paint onto the ground, using large quantities of pesticides and fertilizers, and the throwing of old car batteries into canals has polluted the aquifer and damaged water quality. Unlike surface water pollution, which can be tracked to its source and legally prohibited, groundwater pollution moves slowly through the aquifer, only to show up at some distant point months or years later with no visible signs of its origins.

A third environmental problem traceable to urban sprawl has been the destruction of wildlife species and habitats. Florida's state animal, the Florida panther, has been driven almost to extinction; it is estimated that only thirty panthers remain alive in 1998. Most have been killed while crossing highways that run through their habitats. A whole host of species, including manatees and numerous bird species that live on fish and other wildlife in the state's wetlands, has also been endangered by the state's massive growth. The public's concern about the state's fragile ecostructure has resulted in a few positive developments, most notably the come back of the bald eagle, which had been near extinction in Florida.

A fourth problem has been the degradation of intact ecosystems, notably lakes and bays. Wastes from nearby farms, sugarcane fields, and citrus groves have destroyed some of the state's largest lakes. These agricultural entities have been pushed out of the coastal areas into undeveloped wetlands. Rainwater from farms washes fertilizer into the lakes, causing algae blooms, which deprive the lakes of oxygen and ultimately kill the fish. Similarly, bays in metropolitan areas are polluted by urban runoff and by excessive amounts of fresh water flowing in from canals, which are designed to prevent inland flooding.

### Public Opinion and Voting

The ability of Florida's public officials to deal with the state's environmental and urban problems has been severely restricted by public opinion and politics. It is almost impossible to enact legislation to bring services and taxes into line, to constrain urban sprawl to meet the needs of families, minorities, and the elderly, and to promote public safety. The tendency among pundits is to attribute this situation to public complacency. Florida's voters are said to reflect a lackadaisical, "if it ain't broke, don't fix it" philosophy. But the problem is not so much the public's complacency as it is the sharp partisan divisions. Because the two parties and their supporters disagree fundamentally about the direction to take, Florida struggles to achieve even minimally effective policies.

### Public Attitudes toward Taxes and Services

Constraints on policy makers are most evident in the areas of taxes and services. Surveys have repeatedly shown that Florida voters want public services and facilities expanded but do not want to pay for them. In every year from 1979 to 1994, a majority of respondents have supported increases for combating crime, assisting the elderly, and funding public schools. During more than half of these years, a majority also favored additional expenditures for environmental protection, health-care services, and roads. Only aid to poor families with children generated less than majority support during at least half of the years in question.

On the other hand, antitax sentiment has gained strong support among Florida voters. Although the sales tax remains the most supported form of taxation, opposition to it, nevertheless, has grown. From 1980 to 1994, between 10 and 30 percent of the Florida electorate said that the tax is excessive. Data such as these confirm the view that Floridians want public services and facilities to be improved and expanded, but that they are unwilling to pay the associated cost.

In reality, however, the Florida electorate is not as completely irrational as it would seem. But it is sharply divided. Support for services and opposition to taxes are rooted in two separate coalitions. The antitax coalition is drawn principally from two social classes, while those who support more services and facilities are drawn from a third. The antitax coalition exists among the wealthy and the lower middle class. Retirees can be found in both classes. The wealthy believe that government provides many services that they neither need nor want. The lower middle class opposes taxes because its members resent the benefits that are granted to the poor. They believe, with some justification, that they receive only a modest range of government services and subsidies whereas those who are just one step below them on the economic ladder, and who pay few taxes, receive a wide array of government programs and "handouts."

The protax and proservices coalition is drawn largely from middle-class liberals and moderates. Ironically, they rely on the same logic of self-interest to conclude that taxes and government spending should be maintained if not increased. A sizable proportion of the Florida electorate has expressed support for higher taxes, if those taxes go to the services they value. Middle-class retirees who need health-care services and recreational facilities, and middle-class homeowners who have children attending public schools, are generally progovernment because they believe that government spending will benefit them directly. The problem is that even among these groups there is little or no consensus on the desired services.

PARTISAN TRENDS

The polarization of Florida's electorate is also evident in voter registration trends. Republican voter registration has increased steadily for the past four decades. In 1950 less than 10 percent of the state's voters were registered Republicans, and over 90 percent were Democrats. Today the Republican Party is virtually deadlocked with Democrats in the number of registered voters. Moreover, when voters are asked to indicate their party preference, they are equally divided between the two parties.

The growth of the Republican Party in Florida represents more than a gradual partisan realignment. The Republican resurgence has resulted from the inmigration of several groups—most notably Cubans and midwesterners—who tend to vote Republican. The Republicans also recruited voters directly from the Democratic ranks when the Democratic Party embraced civil rights reform and affirmative action in the 1960s. Conversely, the Democratic Party gained constituents from the retirees who migrated from the Northeast cities (Democratic strongholds), and also enhanced significantly its support among African Americans because of the party's stance on civil rights.

The complexity of Florida's partisan realignment can be seen by examining the geographical distribution of Republican voters. Figure 5 shows the proportion of county voters who were registered Republican in 1996. Growth in Republican voter registration has been concentrated in regions experiencing rapid population growth, almost all of which are located south of Orlando. Most of north Florida and rural, central Florida remain Democratic, although both frequently vote Republican in presidential contests.

Despite the Republican gains, some counties have become less Republican rather than more. Broward County, in particular, has seen a decline in the proportion of Republican registrants since 1970. This trend has developed principally because of the influx of northeastern retirees and the migration from Miami to Ft. Lauderdale of large numbers of Jewish residents, who have historically voted Democratic.

Party affiliation in Florida continues to shift with the population. Although the Republican Party has enjoyed significant gains in the 1980s and 1990s, nothing is certain in a state where the population remains as dynamic and transitory as Florida's.

## Public Policy

Boxed in by a polarized electorate and confronted by rapid urbanization and its attendant problems, state leaders have developed a combination of policies that are consistent with the state's political realities.

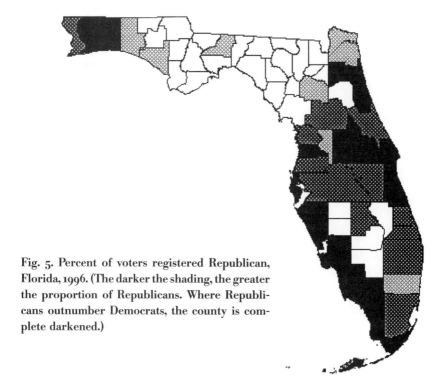

Fig. 5. Percent of voters registered Republican, Florida, 1996. (The darker the shading, the greater the proportion of Republicans. Where Republicans outnumber Democrats, the county is complete darkened.)

Generally referred to as "growth management," its components include a system of state, regional, and local planning within the context of a slowly expanding tax structure. Growth management does not place limits on population growth. Rather, it attempts to anticipate population growth, ensure a more orderly urbanization process, and provide adequate public facilities and services. The concept of managed growth originated in the early 1970s and has evolved over time, but its essentials have remained constant. State, regional, and local units of government are required, through a variety of mechanisms, to plan for growth, to adjust their plans and actions to one another, and to either raise taxes or restrict development as necessary to keep development and public facilities in line.

With this general agreement on growth management policy, the political parties in Florida are left debating issues at the margins. A recurring and important question at all levels of government has been and continues to be how much the state should grow and what level of public services should be provided. Democrats and Republicans answer this question differently because of the different economic interests of their constituencies.

The Democratic Party has advocated a policy of phased urbanization with certain environmental protections and a high level of services and facilities. A minority group in the party has argued for tax reform. They contend that, as each additional person moves into the state, Florida is accumulating a backlog of unmet needs from roads to schools to water and drainage facilities. Those advocating a broad-based tax base and increasing the tax rate to provide facilities and services claim that these adjustments are necessary to preserve the quality of life and also to continue the state's economic development.

This approach to the growth management policy reflects the interests of the state's working classes. Population growth affects one's quality of life differently depending on one's social and economic position. The affluent can generally protect themselves from the undesirable effects of urbanization; they can live in gated communities in the suburbs, shop in safe malls, and go into the cities only when necessary and in the comfort of their automobiles. Those who are less well off usually have busy roads running through their neighborhoods, airplanes flying overhead, landfills built nearby, and other unattractive aspects of urbanization located in or near their neighborhoods. Thus, growth that is inadequately supported by public facilities and services generates greater concern for one class than for another. It is not coincidental that working men and women are one of the key constituent groups in the Democratic Party.

The Republican Party's position on growth management also reflects class interests. Republicans have argued that expanding government at the rate favored by Democrats will stifle growth by raising taxes, creating excessive bureaucracy, and spending state funds wastefully. Republicans favor low taxes and limited government. They argue that Florida's government has grown irresponsibly and unnecessarily, discouraging investment by overtaxing business, undermining hard work by transferring income to the poor, and stifling growth and develop-

**Reubin O'D. Askew and Governor Claude Kirk** mounting the steps of the capitol for Askew's first inaugural as governor. Askew had defeated Kirk, and the difference in style between the flamboyant Kirk and a reserved Askew could not have been more pronounced. Floridians seemed to welcome Askew's style after four years of controversy and turmoil under Kirk. Askew's election also restored the governorship to the Democratic Party. (Florida State Archives)

In 1970 Lawton Chiles walked 1,033 miles in 91 days to dramatize his campaign for the U.S. Senate and earn the nickname "Walkin Lawton." His effort to get beyond television in communicating with citizens influenced the campaign strategies of other candidates in Florida and around the nation. Chiles never lost a campaign for political office. (Florida State Archives)

Governor Reubin O'D. Askew presiding at his first cabinet meeting in January 1971. Seated (*left to right*): Attorney General Robert Shevin, Commissioner of Education Floyd Christian, Commissioner of Agriculture Doyle Connor, Askew, Comptroller Fred Dickinson, Secretary of State Richard Stone, and Treasurer and Insurance Commissioner Tom O'Malley. Askew's administration was ranked as one of the most significant in the twentieth century and Askew was ranked by political scientists as one of the ten best governors in the nation in the century. (Florida State Archives)

Governor Reubin O'D. Askew introducing newly appointed Secretary of State Jessie McCrary to the press and the public in 1978. McCrary was the first African American to serve in the Florida cabinet in the twentieth century. (Florida State Archives)

Representative Gwen Cherry of Miami giving the woman's point of view to Representative Dick Renick of South Miami as the two discuss legislation before the House of Representatives. Cherry was one of the most prominent woman politicians of her generation, serving from 1970 to 1979. She died in an automobile accident in 1979. (Florida State Archives)

Bob Graham worked at 100 different jobs during his gubernatorial campaign in 1976 to win the support of "everyday voters." While the strategy was contrived and designed for publicity, it helped him gain statewide recognition and highlighted the importance of personality over issues in statewide contests in Florida. (Florida State Archives)

Once in office, Bob Graham continued his practice of work days, believing that it kept him in touch with the citizens and aware of their needs and concerns. He also continued this practice when he became a U.S. senator in what has become one of the most innovative ways known of communicating with constituents. Here he worked alongside Willie Lee Rasberry and Samuel De-Loach unloading sod grass in 1979. (Florida State Archives)

Governor Bob Graham met with students and faculty at a Tallahassee high school to mobilize support for his educational initiatives in the 1983 legislative session. He felt strongly that education was central to Florida's economic growth and prosperity. (Florida State Archives)

Governor Bob Graham with members of his cabinet: (*left to right*): Commissioner of Agriculture Doyle Connor (*standing*), Attorney General Jim Smith (*seated*), Commissioner of Education Ralph Turlington (*standing*), Comptroller Gerald Lewis (*standing*), Graham, Insurance Commissioner and Treasurer Bill Gunter (*standing*), and Secretary of State George Firestone. (P. K. Yonge Library of Florida History)

Governor Bob Graham expanded upon Reubin Askew's racial initiatives in Florida, increasing opportunities for black Floridians throughout the state. Here he met in the governor's office with Jesse Jackson, a leading spokesman for racial advancement following the death of the Reverend Martin Luther King, Jr. (Florida State Archives)

Governor Bob Martinez met with reporters to announce the beginning of the Florida Lottery. Revenue from the lottery was to be used to enhance educational funding in the state, but when the recession of 1991–92 reduced state revenues and legislators sought ways to cut state expenditures, the lottery funds replaced regular appropriations for education rather than supplementing them. This development angered many Floridians who felt they had been deliberately misled by legislators on the use of lottery funds. (Florida State Archives)

Senator Toni Jennings (*back to camera*) talking to Senator George Kirkpatrick on the Senate floor in 1987, while Representative Dixie Sansom visited with Senator Bob Crawford. Jennings and Sansom were among those who brought about a women's revolution in the legislature, and Jennings became president of the Senate in 1996. (Florida State Archives)

**Governor Lawton Chiles and Lieutenant Governor Buddy McKay were joined by children and parents in launching their 1994 campaign. Chiles narrowly defeated Jeb Bush, the Republican candidate, in the closest gubernatorial contest in the twentieth century. Their campaign featured the educational and social needs of Florida's children (Florida ranked poorly in several categories in national rankings involving children's services.) (Florida State Archives)**

Miami at the end of the twentieth century stands as the banking capital of the Americas and the commercial center for trade between the Americas. Its dynamic economy and its population diversity are said to be the model for the twenty-first century. (Photo courtesy of Visit Florida)

Men from the Cuban community in Miami gather to play dominoes and to discuss local concerns. Social gatherings of this and other kinds were instrumental in retaining a strong sense of community and building a powerful political infrastructure. (Historical Museum of Southern Florida)

ment with unnecessary regulations. The party advocates strict limits on tax increases by requiring voter approval for any new taxes. The economically affluent generally oppose the growth of government because they are the "taxees" and the "regulatees" and seldom the beneficiaries of the social programs.

Florida politics often seems superficial because of its partisan divisions and because relatively few issues generate political consensus. Both parties would like to capture control of the state government and place their imprint on state politics, but neither has been able to do so in recent years. Instead, because their constituencies are almost equal in size, the parties are balanced on a seesaw, with conservative, rural Democrats at the center shifting support to one side or to the other. From year to year, adjustments are made in taxes and services, depending on economic conditions and public concern about education, health care, and crime. Political campaigns, particularly for statewide offices, usually focus on issues of a symbolic rather than a substantive nature. In the present political environment, Florida politics has been trivialized, and its political leaders campaign for office and often seem to govern by cliché.

### The Failures of Growth Management

The superficial character of Florida politics would not be so frustrating to voters and policy makers if the state's growth management policies dealt effectively with urban and environmental problems, but the policies have proven to be inadequate and at times even counterproductive. Florida has launched three waves of growth management legislation, each one combining a new tax initiative with a new strategy for land use planning and regulation. The first growth management system was created in the 1970s. It established a three-pronged system of land use controls. These controls included a framework of state, regional, and local land use planning; a process for regional review of developments of regional or statewide impact; and a program to designate and protect areas of the state in which unsuitable land development would endanger resources of regional or statewide significance.

At approximately the same time, the tax structure was reformed. Governor Reubin Askew forged a coalition of environmental and business interests in support of a corporate income tax. To gain corporate support for his initiative, Askew threatened to pursue legislation that would tax the net worth of business if voters failed to endorse the corporate income tax. A net worth tax would have been onerous to corporations with large holdings in facilities and equipment, and hence some of Florida's largest companies supported the corporate income tax. To secure the support of environmentalists, Askew supported legislation that would enable the state to begin purchasing large amounts of environmentally sensitive lands if the corporate tax passed. This coalition involving environmentalists and businessmen helped secure voter approval of the 1971 corporate income tax.

The land use policies have been only marginally successful at best, however, especially the planning component. The requirement for local planning had virtually no effect on local land use decisions. When a conflict developed between a local plan and a desired zoning decision, it was often the plan rather than the zoning decision that was adjusted. Many local governments amended their comprehensive plans as often as every few weeks. A rule that required regional and state review of amendments affecting more than 5 percent of a jurisdiction's land was simply circumvented; zoning decisions and amendments were desegregated so that, even though the 5 percent rule applied to them cumulatively, it did not apply to them separately.

By the early 1980s, the problems with growth management efforts in Florida and the need to reform them became increasingly visible. In addition, the expansion of the corporate tax failed to keep up with the rising public sector costs associated with urbanization. As a consequence, the annual legislative sessions from 1984 through 1987 enacted two far-reaching reform packages to Florida's growth management system. One set enhanced the regulatory framework for controlling development by strengthening the local, regional, and state planning process. The other changes involved a significant expansion of the list of items covered by Florida's sales tax. Overall, the objective was to establish a growth management system that would discourage urban sprawl and assure that the public infrastructure would be in place as growth occurred.

Unfortunately, this effort also proved unsuccessful, principally because of the political backlash to the expanded sales tax. In 1986, the legislature decided that the state sales tax would be applied for the first time to purchases of legal, advertising, medical, engineering, accounting, banking, and other services. In the legislative session of 1987, amidst a mounting storm of protest from attorneys, doctors, the media, and others who would be affected, legislators followed through on their intent to extend the sales tax to services. Stunned by the vehemence of the attack and by criticism from members of his own party, Florida's new Republican governor, Bob Martinez, subsequently abandoned his support of the tax and joined other Republicans in the legislature in urging its repeal. After much political haggling, the legislature repealed the services tax and raised the state sales tax from five to six cents. The increase in the sales tax took care of immediate revenue needs but failed to offer a revenue proposal that would address the state's long-term requirements.

The attempt to strengthen the state's system of land use regulation broke down because of the lack of success in developing a meaningful state plan. This plan would have set limits on urban sprawl at the local level, but it proved to be too long, too general, and too inclusive to provide meaningful direction. As a consequence, planning and land use regulation in Florida were left without specific priorities. Nevertheless, local governments remained under a legislative requirement either to disallow new development or to assure that it was provided with adequate public services and facilities. This requirement had the effect of pushing development into rural areas, because public services and facilities there had not yet been overburdened by urbanization. Moreover, because health and human services were exempted from this mandate, county and city expenditures, which were financed heavily by property taxes, were diverted from social services to roads, drainage, and other land use improvements directly associated with construction. Thus, at the risk of oversimplifying the outcome, the net result of the growth management legislation of the 1980s was to raise property taxes on existing residents to pay for roads and drainage so that developers could continue to expand into rural areas.

Florida's third wave of growth management legislation was enacted in the 1990s and appears to be headed toward the same fate as its predecessors. The new law sought to resolve some of the problems in local planning by requiring closer local and regional intergovernmental coordination. Notwithstanding this mandate, meaningful revisions to the state plan have yet to be made, in large part because conflict over changing the plan is too intense. Similarly, implementation of the new system of intergovernmental coordination has been delayed and may be abandoned altogether.

Without a bipartisan agreement on the appropriate balance between taxes and services, Florida has lurched from crisis to crisis. Appropriations are raised only when state revenues increase. When budget cuts are necessitated because of an economic slump or other factors, they are sudden and severe and usually not carefully considered.

By 1995, Glenn W. Robertson, a highly respected former budget director for Democratic governor Bob Graham and Republican governor Bob Martinez, predicted that Florida would face a multi-billion-dollar annual deficit by the end of the decade. "Never before have I seen Florida on the verge of such a fiscal disaster as it now faces," Robertson warned. Within three years, however, Florida had a healthy budget surplus. What had happened?

Several things occurred, all of which worked to the state's financial benefit. The state's rapidly expanding Medicaid rolls, which alone threatened to bankrupt Florida, finally leveled off; welfare rolls declined as the state reformed its welfare laws; and massive cuts in federal spending never materialized. Most important, however, Florida and the nation experienced four very strong years of economic growth, which enhanced state and federal revenues. Florida has been able to tackle school construction, crime, roads, and health care without breaking the treasury.

This economic boom does not mean that Florida's day of reckoning will never come. At some point the economic growth will stall and Florida will be forced to confront fiscal needs that cannot be met by the present tax structure.

## Conclusion

As Florida greets the twenty-first century, it also faces political divisions that threaten the health and well-being of its citizens. This situation has resulted in tax and land use policies that are woefully inadequate and in an unwillingness to address politically sensitive issues. Policy makers have put in place a system of state, regional, and local land use planning that lacks teeth and direction. In a state growing by over 695 residents each day, where development is sprawling indiscriminately over sensitive environmental areas and the very water supply required to support the burgeoning population is at risk, such half-measures are potentially disastrous.

The voters who find this approach acceptable are rural whites, who represent a very small component of the overall populace. Although they are registered Democrats, they prefer low taxes because they have little need for urban services and because their income levels are generally low. For them, a tight budget that is designed to keep their taxes low and support only essential public services is just fine. Similarly, they have little interest in a restrictive land use policy. After all, many farmers and others with rural landholdings hope to be able to sell their land in the future to developers and thus profit from suburbanization.

Other voters in the state, however, are quite dissatisfied, regardless of which party they support. Conservatives believe that taxes are too high and that Florida government, especially the agencies involved in land use regulation, has become too restrictive and too bureaucratic. Liberals believe that the state's public services and facilities are inadequate and that its environmental resources are being destroyed.

These political divisions prevent sound policies from being developed in Florida that will meet the needs of a rapidly expanding population and that will protect the environment that attracted these residents to Florida in the first place. The only way to break the cycle, if indeed it can be broken, is to find a way of forging a centrist civic culture that goes beyond partisanship and speaks to the critical needs of the state and its citizens and forges a consensus behind them.

# 5 Reflections on State Government in Florida

As Florida enters the new millennium, it confronts issues that are even more significant for its future than those it faced at the beginning of the twentieth century. Population growth by itself threatens the state's ability to manage its resources and secure its fragile environment for future generations. The absence of a statewide identity as a result of massive growth in the post–World War II era has impaired the state's ability to forge consensus around critical issues. Communities have enough difficulty building a local consensus among natives and newcomers without reaching out to neighboring cities.

The increasing diversity of the state also poses special needs and concerns for local communities. While most Floridians refuse to restrict the rights of these new citizens or erect barriers to limit their involvement in civic affairs, as they did to black Floridians a hundred years earlier, they have also been unwilling to acknowledge that diversity can be a positive development for the state. Floridians from the northern and central regions, for example, see little in common with south Florida, in large measure because of the diversity of its population. As a consequence, residents from these two regions have little interest in addressing the needs of south Florida. Florida's place as a retirement home for the nation's senior citizens has also narrowly defined community life and state politics. The state's senior citizens have used the vote and their political muscle to influence significantly which issues will be addressed and which will not. Their concerns have less to do with the needs of the state as a whole and more to do with the particular concerns of their age group.

These changes in the size and character of Florida's population have dramatically reshaped the state. If you had visited Florida in 1900 and returned in 2000, you would not recognize it. Indeed, it is not the same state. Symbolizing the degree to which the state has changed, it now serves both as the port of embarkation for the Caribbean and South American and for the exploration of the universe.

And yet, despite these dramatic changes, the structure of state politics has changed remarkably little in the past hundred years. The governor still finds himself and his office hamstrung by constitutional strictures that were imposed in the nineteenth century as a reaction to the radical Republican government following the Civil War. This collegial form of government, known as the cabinet system, was designed to limit the power of the executive branch. But it is largely unchanged. During such major crises as the Great Depression and World War II, Florida's chief executive has been limited to whatever actions he could persuade his fellow cabinet members to pursue. For a small, frontier-like state in the nineteenth century, this may have made political sense; for a large, diverse state confronting the many problems of the twentieth century, this nineteenth century structure makes no sense.

While the structure of government remains fundamentally unchanged in Florida, its politics has changed significantly in the late twentieth century. The rise of the Republican Party has been dramatic. In the brief seventeen years from 1980 to 1997, Republicans have captured control of both houses of the legislature, one-half the seats in the cabinet, and over half the congressional delegation.

The emergence of the Republican Party, however, has not brought about any comparable change in the direction and organization of state government. The state still remains fragmented by its enormous population growth and divided by age and diversity. The fundamentally conservative nature of state politics has, if anything, become even more conservative. Florida politicians have never been advocates of big government. And that has certainly remained true in the era of Republican ascendancy. The Florida Republican Party believes that most state programs can be more efficiently and effectively provided by the private sector. Although this view may seem radically new, it is not for Florida. This conservative view of government dominated state politics for much of the twentieth century, and it is one with which Floridians still seem quite comfortable.

The basic conservatism of Florida voters has remained remarkably constant despite the dramatic social and economic changes that have occurred over the past century, and this philosophical view of government has been reinforced by recent demographic changes. The state's senior citizens, for example, generally oppose new tax initiatives or government programs that will require additional spending, because they fear it will cut into their fixed budgets. Moreover, they are generally satisfied with their quality of life and with the services they receive from the state and federal government, and so are reluctant to consider any significant change in the operation of government.

Florida's conservative impulse has also been fueled by the continued influx of new residents. More than one-half of the current population has moved into Florida since 1970. Few of these people understand the critical issues confronting the state. As a consequence, they tend to adopt a conservative political outlook, because they have little sense of the needs of the state as a whole and because they are consumed by pressures of adjusting to a new life in a new community. Symptomatic of the fundamental conservatism of Floridians, voters balked at a major effort to reform the Constitution in 1978, and they have passed a series of citizen initiatives designed to limit the ability of the state to raise revenues and pursue new programs.

The political conservatism of state residents has been strengthened further by the failure of many of the federal reforms of the 1960s, the enormous debt incurred by the federal government in the 1980s and early 1990s, and the general distrust of politicians that has escalated in this country since the 1960s. These developments have fundamentally shaped the way many Floridians view government. As a consequence, it is likely that the conservative political ideology that dominates state politics will continue to do so for the foreseeable future.

As Florida enters the new century, its development continues to be shaped fundamentally by issues related to growth. Most Floridians see growth as a good thing because it brings jobs, development, and prosperity to the state. And yet unregulated growth represents the major threat to the state's future. No state, even one as large as Florida, can continue to accommodate 2 million or more new residents every decade without experiencing a profound impact on its quality of life. Moreover, Florida's fragile environment and its water supply, especially in south Florida, are constantly threatened by uncontrolled growth.

Floridians recognize that growth will continue to be a problem, because the reasons that brought them to the state will persuade others to follow. But as roads become increasingly clogged and schools more congested, and as the water supply faces intrusion by salt water, more and more Floridians are seeking ways to regulate growth to protect the environment that attracted them in the first place.

If Florida is to secure the economic future it so desperately sought for much of the twentieth century, it will have to find a new way to come to terms with growth. To do so, state and local governments must be able and willing to regulate growth and limit or prevent its harmful effects. If they do not do this, Florida will suffocate economically and environmentally.

At the time of this writing, however, Floridians have such a negative attitude toward political leadership that they do not trust their politicians to provide suitable direction for the state. Most politicians who wish to retain office avoid such controversial issues as population growth and environmental protection. Moreover, the two major parties, currently deadlocked in a battle for political control of the state, have addressed these issues only at the margins for fear they will undermine their political aspirations. Ironically, Floridians clearly value orderly and well-regulated communities, as is evidenced by those with sufficient wealth who flock to gated subdivisions throughout the state. But these gated communities will only provide short-term relief if the communities that are outside the gates are allowed to deteriorate.

Even if Floridians and their political leaders could agree to address these matters, the state presently lacks the political infrastructure to resolve them effectively. The challenge confronting Florida in the twenty-first century is to seek solutions to the problems created by growth and at the same time ensure the state's economic advancement and continued opportunity for its citizens. The boom of the late twentieth century sits atop a shaky foundation in Florida. Solidifying that foundation for the twenty-first century depends on the state's political leadership and the political will of the people.

As long as Floridians remain suspicious of their political leaders, however, they will prevent them from developing a systematic approach to growth management and from taking steps to secure a better future for this and subsequent generations. Florida does not need to construct a massive bureaucracy to address the problems that threaten its future, but its citizens must allow its leaders to govern and to help plan for the next generation. Perhaps that will happen in the twenty-first century, but as Floridians say goodbye to the old, they appear unwilling to let go of their old ways of doing things. For state politics, that means the continuation of a limited chief executive and limited state government. Thus, as the dawn rises on the new millennium, Floridians remain unwilling to abandon the politics that were set in place in the nineteenth century. The challenges the state faces today are much different from those it faced at the beginning of the twentieth century, but its ability to address them is no less certain.

# Bibliography

Arsenault, Raymond. "The End of the Long Hot Summer: The Air Conditioner and Southern Culture." *Journal of Southern History* 6, no. 4 (November 1984): 597–628.

———. *St. Petersburg and the Florida Dream, 1888–1950*. Norfolk: Donning Co., 1988.

Bernard, Richard M., and Bradley R. Rice, eds. *Sunbelt Cities: Politics and Growth since World War II*. Austin: University of Texas Press, 1983.

Blake, Nelson M. *Land into Water—Water into Land: A History of Water Management in Florida*. Tallahassee: Florida State University Press, 1980.

Bouvier, Leon F., and Bob Weller. *Florida in the 21st Century: The Challenge of Population Growth*. Washington, D.C.: Center for Immigration Studies, 1992.

Button, James. *Blacks and Social Change: Impact of the Civil Rights Movement in Southern Communities*. Princeton: Princeton University Press, 1989.

Carr, Patrick. *Sunshine States: Wild Times and Extraordinary Lives in the Land of Gators, Guns, and Grapefruits*. Garden City, N.Y.: Doubleday, 1990.

Cash, William T. *A History of the Democratic Party in Florida*. Tallahassee: Florida Democratic Historical Foundation, 1936.

Chalmers, David. "The Ku Klux Klan in the Sunshine State: The 1920s." *Florida Historical Quarterly* 42, no. 3 (January 1964): 209–15.

Colburn, David R. *Racial Change and Community Crisis: St. Augustine, Florida, 1877–1980*. New York: Columbia University Press, 1985. Reprint, Gainesville: University Press of Florida, 1991.

Colburn, David R., and Richard K. Scher. *Florida's Gubernatorial Politics in the Twentieth Century*. Gainesville: University Presses of Florida, 1980.

Colburn, David R., and Jane L. Landers, eds. *The African American Heritage of Florida*. Gainesville: University Press of Florida, 1995.

Dauer, Manning, ed. *Florida's Politics and Government*. Gainesville: University Presses of Florida, 1980.

deHaven-Smith, Lance. *Environmental Concern in Florida and the Nation*. Gainesville: University Presses of Florida, 1989.

———. *The Florida Voter*. Tallahassee: LeRoy Collins Center, 1997.

Douglas, Marjory Stoneman. *The Everglades: River of Grass*. New York: Rinehart, 1947.

Dye, Thomas R. *Public Policy in Florida: A Fifty-State Perspective*. Tallahassee: Policy Sciences Program, Florida State University, 1992.

Fiedler, Tom, and Lance deHaven-Smith. *Almanac of Florida Politics 1998*. Dubuque, Iowa: Kendall/Hunt, 1997.

Fjellman, Stephen M. *Vinyl Leaves: Walt Disney World and America*. Boulder, Colo.: Westview, 1992.

Flynt, Wayne. *Cracker Messiah: Governor Sidney J. Catts of Florida*. Baton Rouge: Louisiana State University Press, 1977.

———. *Duncan Upshaw Fletcher: Dixie's Reluctant Progressive*. Tallahassee: Florida State University Press, 1971.

Franklin, John Hope. *From Slavery to Freedom: A History of Negro Americans*. 4th ed. New York: Alfred A. Knopf, 1974.

Gannon, Michael V. *Florida: A Short History*. Gainesville: University Press of Florida, 1993.

———, ed. *The New History of Florida*. Gainesville: University Press of Florida, 1996.

Hall, Kermit L., and James W. Ely, Jr., eds. *An Uncertain Tradition: Constitutionalism and the History of the South*. Athens: University of Georgia Press, 1989.

Havard, William C., and Loren P. Beth. *The Politics of Mis-representation: Rural-Urban Conflict in the Florida Legislature*. Baton Rouge: Louisiana State University Press, 1962.

Huckshorn, Robert J., ed. *Government and Politics in Florida*. Gainesville: University Press of Florida, 1991; 2d edition, 1998.

Ingalls, Robert P. *Urban Vigilantes in the New South: Tampa, 1882–1936*. Knoxville: University of Tennessee Press, 1988. Reprint, Gainesville: University Press of Florida, 1993.

Key, V. O., Jr. *Southern Politics in the State and Nation*. New York: Vintage Press, 1949.

Kallina, Edward. *Claude Kirk and the Politics of Confrontation*. Gainesville: University Press of Florida, 1993.

Kersey, Harry A., Jr. *The Florida Seminoles and the New Deal, 1933–1942*. Gainesville: University Presses of Florida, 1989.

Kluger, Richard. *Simple Justice: The History of Brown v. Board of Education and Black America's Struggle for Equality*. New York: Alfred A. Knopf, 1976.

Kousser, J. Morgan. *The Shaping of Southern Politics: Suffrage Restriction and the Establishment of the One-Party South, 1880–1910*. New Haven: Yale University Press, 1974.

Lawson, Steven. *Black Ballots: Voting Rights in the South, 1944–1969*. New York: Columbia University Press, 1976.

McGovern, James R. *Anatomy of a Lynching: The Killing of Claude Neal*. Baton Rouge: Louisiana State University Press, 1982.

Miller, Randall M., and George E. Pozzetta, eds. *Shades of the Sunbelt: Essays on Ethnicity, Race, and the Urban South*. Westport, Conn.: Greenwood Press, 1988. Reprint, Gainesville: University Press of Florida, 1989.

Mohl, Raymond A. "Miami: The Ethnic Cauldron." In *Sunbelt Cities: Politics and Growth Since World War II*, edited by Richard M. Bernard and Bradley R. Rice. Austin: University of Texas Press, 1983.

———. "Race and Space in the Modern City: Interstate 95 and the Black Community in Miami." In *Urban Policy in Twentieth-Century America*, edited by Arnold R. Hirsch and Raymond A. Mohl. New Brunswick, N.J.: Rutgers University Press, 1993.

———, ed. *Searching for the Sunbelt: Historical Perspectives on a Region*. Knoxville: University of Tennessee Press, 1990.

Mormino, Gary R. "G.I. Joe Meets Jim Crow: Racial Violence and Reform in World War II Florida." *Florida Historical Quarterly* 73, no. 1 (July 1994): 23–42.

Mormino, Gary R., and George E. Pozzetta. *The Immigrant World of Ybor City: Italians and Their Latin Neighbors in Tampa, 1885–1985.* Urbana: University of Illinois Press, 1987.

Morris, Allen. *The Florida Handbook, 1997–1998.* Tallahassee: Peninsular Publishing Co., 1997.

Nolan, David. *Fifty Feet in Paradise: The Booming of Florida.* New York: Harcourt Brace Jovanovich, 1984.

Portes, Alejandro, and Alex Stepick. *City on the Edge: The Transformation of Miami.* Berkeley: University of California Press, 1993.

Price, Hugh. *The Negro and Southern Politics: A Chapter of Florida History.* New York: New York University Press, 1957.

Proctor, Samuel. *Napoleon Bonaparte Broward: Florida's Fighting Democrat.* Gainesville: University Press of Florida, 1950; reprint, 1993.

Richardson, Joe M. *The Negro in the Reconstruction of Florida, 1865–1877.* Tallahassee: Florida State University Press, 1965.

Rogers, William Warren. *Outposts on the Gulf: Saint George Island and Apalachicola from Early Exploration to World War II.* Gainesville: University Presses of Florida, 1986.

Smith, Charles U., ed. *The Civil Rights Movement in Florida and the United States.* Tallahassee: Father and Son Publishing, 1993.

Shofner, Jerrell H. "Custom, Law, and History: The Enduring Influence of Florida's 'Black Code'." *Florida Historical Quarterly* 57, no. 3 (January 1977): 277–98.

———. "Florida and Black Migration." *Florida Historical Quarterly* 57, no. 3 (January 1979): 267–88.

———. *Nor Is It Over Yet: Florida in the Era of Reconstruction, 1865–1877.* Gainesville: University Presses of Florida, 1974.

Tebeau, Charlton W. *A History of Florida.* Coral Gables: University of Miami Press, 1971; revised 1980.

Tindall, George B. *The Emergence of the New South, 1913–1945.* Baton Rouge: Louisiana State University Press, 1967.

Vance, Linda D. *May Mann Jennings, Florida's Genteel Activist.* Gainesville: University Presses of Florida, 1980.

Wagy, Thomas R. *Governor LeRoy Collins: Spokesman of the New South.* Tuscaloosa: University of Alabama Press, 1985.

# Index

*Note: Page references in italics refer to photographs.*

ad valorem taxes. *See* property tax

affirmative action, 130

African Americans: in government, 82, *134;* in Great Depression, *54;* jobs for, 17–18, 37, 123; as judges, *100;* neighborhoods and schools of, 122–24; oppression of, xii, 9, 18–19, 30–31, 37; outmigration of, 17–18, 31; political participation of, 43, 130; population of, 3, 31; rights denied to, xii, 10–12, 16, 18–19; violence against, xii, 18, 19, 37, 41; voting by, 18–19, 37, 41–42, 47–48, 51; in World War I, 16–17; in World War II, 35–37. *See also* civil rights movement; race; segregation

Agricultural Adjustment Act, 30

agriculture: black workers and, 18; commissioners of, 86–87; diminished influence of, 50, 123; federal assistance for, 30–31; pests in, 17, 29; promotion of, 11–12; vs. railroad interests, 14; water pollution from, 126–28

Aid to Families with Dependent Children (AFDC), 110

air conditioning, introduction of, 34–35

Air Force, bases for, 33–34, 103–4

Akerman, Alex, *30*

American Association of Retired Persons (AARP), 50

Apollo XI, *99*

Appropriations Committee, 81, 82–83, 84

Askew, Gov. Reubin O'D.: activities of, *99,* 115–16, *134;* campaign and election of, 65, 72–73; on casino gambling, 48, 113; environmental issues under, 67–68; inauguration of, *133;* petitions of, 68, 111; on reform commission, 89; on tax reform, 142

attorney general, function of, 87, 88

automobiles: Florida type of, *22;* governor's use of, *24;* impact of, *21.* *See also* roads; tourist camps

*Baker* v. *Carr,* 44

balanced budget requirement, 47, 48, 84

Ball, Ed, *96*

banks: failures of, 29; hostility toward, 7–8; Miami as center for, 50, *140*

Barron, Dempsey, 82, 113–14

beaches: automobiles on, *21;* segregation on, *94*

bill, definition of, 81. *See also* legislation
Bill of Rights (Florida), 45
Black Codes, 9. *See also* Jim Crow laws; segregation
blacks. *See* African Americans
Board of Regents, appointments to, 90
boards: appointments to, 90–91; function of, 88–89; patronage on, 106
Boca Raton, minority neighborhoods in, 122
Broward, Gov. Napoleon Bonaparte, 14–15, 16, 22
Broward County: local government in, 105; political delegation of, 83; politics in, 72, 73, 91, 130; population of, 121; schools in, 106, 123; urbanization in, 104
*Brown v. Board of Education*, 39–40, 59
Bryant, Gov. C. Farris, 40–41, 93, 95, 99
budget: annual development of, 84–85; approach to, 116–17; commission on, 88; crisis mentality toward, 144; requirement for balanced, 47, 48, 84. *See also* finances; taxes
Budget Commission, 88
Burns, Gov. W. Haydon, 40–41, 99
buses (city), desegregation of, 93
Bush, Jeb, 70, 73
Business and Professional Regulation, Department of, 90. *See also* corporations
busing: opposition to, 52, 65; resistance to, 123; support for, 68

cabinet system: appointments to, 80–81, 86; characteristics of, 5, 86; continued in 1968 Constitution, 46–47; establishment of, 10, 85–86; functions of, 88–89; political parties and, 73, 86–87; power in, 86–87; proposal to eliminate, 113–14; terms for, 85–87, 89–90. *See also* boards; commissions; executive branch; governors
Caldwell, Gov. Millard F.: activities of, 56, 58, 99; cabinet relations of, 87;

economic development under, 34–35; government reorganization under, 36; legacy of, 68; race relations under, 36
California: Florida compared to, 49–50; immigration to, 103; population in, 120
campaigns: children as issue in, *139*; civil rights, 35, 41, *94*, *95*; cost of, 70; environmental, 68; SCLC, 41, *94*, *95*; state limits on, 70. *See also* elections; voting; *specific governors and U.S. presidents*
canal, opposition to, 66–67, *96*
Cape Canaveral, economic impact of, *99*, 104
Caribbean region, migrants from, 2, 3, 43, 50, 103, 121
Carlton, Gov. Doyle, 29
Carr, Marjorie, 67, *96*
Carter, Jimmy, 51, 73
casino gambling, petition on, 48, 68, 111, 113
Castor, Betty, 67
Catholic Church, 20, 51
cattle ranching, diminished influence of, 50
Catts, Gov. Sidney J., 18, 20, 24
Central America, migrants from, 2, 3, 43, 50, 103, 121
central region: characteristics of, 3, 146–47; politics of, 130
Charlotte County, population of, 120
Cherry, Gwen, *135*
Childers, W. D., 83
Chiles, Gov. Lawton: appointments by, 81, 91; campaign and election of, 65–66, 70, 72–73, *133*, *139*; government reform under, 89; legacy of, 68; rhetoric of, 73; as U.S. senator, 87
Christian, Floyd, *134*
"Cincinnati factor," 33
Circuit courts: appointments to, 101–2; role of, 91, 101
citizens: indifference of, xii; local government authority and, 79; petition

process and, 4, 48–49, 68, 110–12; responsibilities of, ix–x. *See also* minorities; public; public opinion; senior citizens; voting

Citizens Commission on Cabinet Reform, 89

Citrus, Department of, 90

citrus industry: black workers and, 18; fruit fly infestation and, 29; water pollution from, 127–28

city government: bus desegregation and, *93*; downtowns vs. suburbs and, 122; service provision and, 108–9; structure of, 104. *See also* local governments

city manager system, 15, 104

Civil Rights Act (1964), 41

civil rights movement: campaigns for, 41, *93, 94, 95*; coalition for, 72–73; emergence of, xiii, 40–41; partisan support for, 130

Civil War, Florida's role in, 8–11. *See also* southern culture

climate, drawbacks of, 34. *See also* hurricanes

coastline, environmental campaign for, 68. *See also* beaches

Collier County, population of, 120

Collins, Gov. LeRoy: activities of, *61, 62, 99*; on cabinet elimination proposal, 113–14; cabinet relations of, 87; campaigns of, 51, 52, *58, 59*; legacy of, 68; opposition to, xiii; on race relations, 39–40, 41; on reapportionment, 38–39

Commerce, Department of, 34, 90. *See also* corporations; industrialization

commissions: for agriculture, 86–87; appointments to, 90–91; county government, 106–7; on education, 67, 88–89; function of, 88–89; on government reform, 89; on taxes and budget, 88, 112. *See also* Constitution Revision Commission

committees: on appropriations, 81, 82–83, 84; control of, 82–83; on judicial

nominations, 101; responsibilities of, 81; on rules, 81, 83; on taxes and finances, 81

community action agencies (CAAs), 109–10

Community Affairs, Department of, 90

Cone, Gov. Fred, 29–30, *53*

Connor, Doyle, 87, *134, 137*

constitution (general): citizen amendments for, 4, 110–12; convention for revision of, 111; courts' role in upholding, 92

Constitution (1839), 7–8

Constitution (1865), 9

Constitution (1868), 9–10

Constitution (1885): influences on, 10; opposition to, 45; provisions in, xiii, 10, 32, 85–86

Constitution (1968): adoption of, 45, 74, 78; amendments to, 48, 80, 112–15; context for, 44–45, 88–89; ethics code in, 111; local governments vested in, 102, 106–7; provisions in, 45–48, 79, 84, 85, 91, 108; revision process for, 110–12, 148; shortcomings of, 110

Constitution Revision Commission: amendments proposed by, 112–13; for 1968 Constitution, 44–45

construction industry, role of, 50

corporations: denunciation of, 20; influence of, *96*; international, 1, 35, 76; taxes on, 68, 142

Corrections, Department of, 90. *See also* judiciary system

counties: delegations from, 83; government structure in, 104–5, 106–7; home-rule charters for, 106–7; responsibilities of, 104; services delivered by, 108–9; taxes collected by, 108. *See also* local governments

County courts: appointments to, 101–2; role of, 91, 101

courts. *See* judiciary system; Supreme Court (Fla.)

Cramer, William, 65

Crawford, Bob, *138*

crime: funds for combating, 128, 144; Kirk's approach to, 65; migration and, 13; against tourists, 75. *See also* judiciary system; prisons

Cross-Florida Barge Canal, 66–67, *96*

Cuban Americans: influence of, 50–51, 124; migration of, 3; politics and, 82, 130

Dade County: local government in, 102, 105; politics in, 72; population of, 50–51, 121; urbanization in, 104

D'Alemberte, Sandy, 113–14

Daytona Beach: city manager system in, 15; population of, 120

Democratic Party: on constitutional revision, 45; diminished influence of, 51–52, *61*, 69–74; divisions in, 12–13, 31, 69; dominance of, 12, 28, 30, 31–33, 52, 86–87; growth management and, 132, 145; influences on, 4; migrants in, 33; percentage registered as, 129–31; Populist movement opposed by, 11–12; racial caste system of, 10–11, 40–41; revitalization of, 65–66, 68; third-party challenge to, 20

Dickinson, Fred, *134*

Disston, Hamilton, 10

District Courts of Appeal: appointments to, 47; role of, 91, 92

diversity: challenges of, 146–47; importance of, x, 1; migration's impact in, 3, 43–44, 49–51; political implications of, 4, 119; reflected in legislature, 78

Douglas, Marjory Stoneman, 67, *96*

drainage: of Everglades, 14; funds for, 143; special districts for, 105

duPont, Jessie, *96*

Duval County, local government in, 102, 105

East Florida, statehood and, 7

economic development: context for, 33–37, 40–42; control of, 141–44; education linked to, 68; homestead exemption and, 28; NASA's impact on, *99*, 104; Progressive movement and, 13–15; race relations and, 38–42; support for, 15–16, 51; urban sprawl and, 122; in World War II, 31–33, *55*. *See also* real estate development

Economic Opportunity Act (1964), 109

economy: boom and bust cyle in (1920–1940), 28–31; development of (1890–1925), 11–20; hurricane's impact on, *26*, 75; population changes and, 50; post–Civil War problems in, 9–10; problems in (1990s), 75–76; recent boom in, 144. *See also* economic development; international business; tourism

education: attitudes toward, 75; commissioners of, 67, 88–89; commitment to public, 14; economic development linked to, 68; funding for, 106, 116–17, 129, *138*. *See also* schools

Eight Is Enough amendment, 80

Elder Affairs, Department of, 90

elections: constitutional amendments on ballots for, 110–11, 114–15; primary system for, 12–13; women running in, 19. *See also* campaigns; presidential elections; voting; *specific governors*

environmental concerns: attitudes toward, 145; development privileged over, 15–16; funds for, 128; group organized on, 20, *96*; interest in, 66–68; land purchases and, 142; promotional campaigns for, 68; women involved in, 20, 67, *96*. *See also* natural resources

Environmental Land and Water Management Act, 67–68

Environmental Protection, Department of, 90

Escambia County, local government in, 105

ethnicity. *See* African Americans; Cuban

Americans; diversity; Jewish Americans; minorities
Everglades: development of, 14–15; environmental campaign for, 68; National Park created in, 58; threats to, 126–27
executive branch: budget development and, 84; expansion of, 36; fragmentation of, 79, 85–87, 90; reform of, 88–90; responsibility for, 87–88; structure of, 5, 46–47, 85–86. See also boards; cabinet system; commissions; governors

facilities: funding for, 124–28; growth management and, 132. See also services
Farmer's Alliance, 11–12
federal government: financial assistance from, 30–31, 33, 34, 58; grants-in-aid from, 109–10; racial policies and, 35–36, 41–42; Reagan's approach to, 69–70; role of, 102–4; on state apportionment, 44; transportation construction by, 34
fence law, 35
Finance and Tax Committee, 81
finances: attitudes toward, 75; balanced budget requirement for, 47, 48, 84; committees on, 81, 82–83, 84, 112; complexity of, 5; constitutional amendments related to, 115; economic development and, 14–15, 33; of judicial system, 91–92; for public facilities and services, 124–28; state debt and, 9, 149. See also banks; budget; taxes
fire protection, 105, 110
Flagler, Henry, 10, 15, 23
flood protection, 106. See also water management
Florida: as bellwether state, 1–3, 76; challenges for, 146–50; distinctiveness of, 3–5, 31; modernization of, 49–52, 65–66; motto of, 2; statehood of, 7, 8; transformation of, xii–xiv, 1–3, 74–76.

See also economic development; growth management; local governments; politics; regionalism; state government; specific cities and counties
Florida A&M University, 98
Florida Bar Association, 47, 101
Florida Defenders of the Environment, 96
Florida East Coast Railroad, 15, 23
Florida (State) League of Women Voters, 19–20
Florida State University, xiii
Forman, Hamilton, 91
Ft. Lauderdale: environmental degradation in, 126; 1926 hurricane in, 26
Ft. Meyers, population of, 30
Fuller, Edna Giles, 19

Gainesville: politics in, 73; tourist camp near, 25
gender, social construction of, 19. See also women
General Appropriations Bill/Act, 81, 90
Gilchrist, Gov. Albert, 15, 23
government. See federal government; local governments; state government
governors: appointments by, 47, 80–81, 86, 90–91, 101, 106, 112; budget development and, 84–85; cabinet relations of, 86–87; impeachment process for, 80; line-item veto for, 84–85, 90; nepotism of, 24; power of, 46–47, 49, 86, 90–91, 115; responsibilities of, 87–88, 91; restrictions on, xiii, 7, 10, 47, 78–79, 85–86, 116, 147; as state spokesperson, 91; terms for, 85, 87. See also cabinet system; executive branch; specific governors
Graham, Gov. Bob: activities of, 68–69, 136; cabinet of, 137; campaign and election of, 65–66, 70, 72–73, 135; on migrants, 33; racial initiatives under, 137; as U.S. senator, 87; workdays of, 65–66, 135, 136

grants-in-aid (federal), 109–10
Gray, R. A., 87
Great Depression: African Americans in, 54; Cone's approach to, 53; precursor to, 28–29
Great Society programs, 109–10
growth management: challenges for, 149–50; concept of, 131; environmental degradation and, 126–28; failures of, 141–44, 145; funding issues and, 124–26; government modernization and, 79; public attitudes and, 128–30; public policy and, 130–32, 141; reform of, 142–43; unincorporated areas and, 107–8; urban sprawl and, 119–24. See also economic development; real estate development; water management
Gunter, Bill, 69, 137
Gurney, Edward, 52, 66

Hardee, Gov. Cary, 25, 28
Hatchett, Joseph W., 100
Hawkins, Paula, 69, 70
health care, funds for, 103, 116–17, 128–29, 144
Hernando County, population of, 120
high technology manufacturing: importance of, 50; water pollution from, 127
Hillsborough County, local government in, 105
Holland, Gov. Spessard: activities of, 56, 58, 61, 63; cabinet relations of, 87; federal cooperation and, 34; inauguration of, 54
homestead exemption, 28, 125
hospitals: boards for, 90–91; special districts for, 91, 105
House of Representatives: budget responsibilities of, 84–85; powers of, 80–81; reapportionment and, 38–39; Speaker of, 81–83, 84, 116; staff of, 83–84; term limits for, 80, 89–90; women in, 19, 135, 138
Hurricane Andrew, 75, 88

hurricanes, effects of, 26, 29, 75, 88

immigration. See migration
income tax: corporate, 68, 142; personal, 48, 74, 125
industrialization: Progressive movement and, 13–15; water pollution from, 127
international business: influence of, 1; state's recruitment of, 35, 76
Interstate 95, development of, 124
Islandia, population of, 104

Jackson, Andrew, 21
Jacksonville: FDR's visit to, 27; local government in, 105; military in, 33–34; population of, 28, 104; urban sprawl of, 122
Jacksonville, St. Augustine & Halifax Railway Company, 23
Jennings, May Mann, 19–20, 22, 67
Jennings, Toni, 67, 138
Jennings, Gov. William Sherman, 14–15, 19, 22
Jewish Americans: activism of, 51; politics of, 130
Jim Crow laws, xiii, 11. See also Black Codes; segregation
Johns, Gov. Charley E., 40, 58, 99
Johnson, Lyndon B.: appointments by, 62; dissatisfaction with, 46, 52; Great Society of, 109–10; support for, 51
judges: African Americans as, 100; terms for, 47, 92, 101–2
Judicial Nominating Committee, 101
judiciary system: levels in, 91–92, 101–2; reform of, 47, 74, 91–92, 102. See also judges; Supreme Court (Fla.)
justices of the peace, elimination of, 102
Juvenile Justice, Department of, 90

Kennedy, John F., 62, 63
Kennedy Space Center, 99, 104
Key, V. O., Jr.: on distinctiveness, 3–4, 31; on politics, 13, 31–33

Key West: local government in, 106; population of, 9
King, Rev. Martin Luther, Jr., 41, *94*, *95*
Kirk, Gov. Claude: activities of, *97*, *98*, *133*; on constitutional revision, 45; election of, 52; environmental issues under, 66–67; voters alienated by, 52, 65, 66
Kirkpatrick, George, *138*
Kogan, Gerald, 102
Ku Klux Klan, 17, 37, *61*

labor: for military base construction, 33–34; "right-to-work" provision and, 45; treatment of black veterans as, 37; unemployment level and, 75–76; urban sprawl's impact on, 123. *See also* agriculture; labor movement
labor movement, *23*
laws: citizen amendments for, 4; definition of, 81; resign to run, 4. *See also* legislation
Legal Affairs, Department of, 88
legislation: definitions of, 81; growth management type of, 141–44; special districts established by, 105
Legislative Reorganization Act (1969), 49, 79
legislators: positions of power for, 81–84, 116, *138*; resign to run law for, 4
legislature: in budget process, 84–85, 116–17; in constitutional amendment process, 110–12; homestead exemption adopted by, 28, 125; House vs. Senate in, 80–81; influences on, *64*; politicization of process in, 75–76; power in, 46, 49, 81–84; on reform commission's recommendations, 89; reputation of, 79–80; sessions of, 78, 85; staff system for, 4, 49, 83–84; structure of, 7; tax debates in, 29. *See also* committees; House of Representatives; reapportionment; Senate
Leon County, local government in, 105

Lewis, Gerald, *137*
Liberty City, 124
lieutenant governor: office established for, 46; terms for, 85
line-item veto, in legislative process, 84–85, 90
"Little Cabinet," 90
local governments: complexity of, 5, 107; consensus in, 146; constitutional amendments related to, 115; fragmentation of, 104–5, 107–10; growth management planning by, 131, 142–44; home rule for, 48, 106–7; modernization of, 78–79; officers of, 78–79; overlap in, 107, 108–9; problems with, 102; restrictions on, 48; structure of, 104–7. *See also* city government; counties; rural areas; urban areas
Logan, Willie, 82
Lottery, Department of, 90, *138*
Lowry, Sumter L., *59*
lumber industry. *See* timber industry
lynchings, xii, 18

Mack, Connie, 69–70, 71–72
Manatee County, schools seized in, 52, 65, *98*
Mann, A. S., *22*
Margolis, Gwen, 67
Martin, Gov. John, *26*, *27*
Martinez, Gov. Bob: appointments by, 71; election of, 69–70, 91; on Lottery, *138*; on reform commission, 89; on taxes on services, 71, 143
Mayo, Nathan, 86
mayoral system, 104
McCarty, Gov. Dan, 36, *58*
McCaskill, Myrtice Vera, 19
McCrary, Jessie, *134*
McKay, Buddy, *139*
media: vs. direct voter contact, 65–66; in elections, 52, 65, *93*; on service tax, 71
Medicaid, 75, 103, 110, 144

Miami: as banking and financial center, 50, *140;* hurricane in, 26, 29; influence of, 3; military in, 34; population of, 28, 31, 104, 120–21; road development in, 124; urban sprawl of, 122

Miami Beach: military in, 33–34, *55;* population of, 121; property values in, 28

Middle Florida, statehood and, 7

migration: of African Americans to north, 17–18, 31; challenges of, 149; "Cincinnati factor" in, 33; federal and state roles in, 103; of military personnel, 33–34, 35, 74; political impact of, 130; shifting population and, 32–33; southern culture and, 3–4, 7; urban sprawl and, 120–21, 123

military: bases and training for, 34, *55;* economic development and, 33–34, 103–4; migration and, 33–34, 35, 74

Military Reconstruction Acts, 9–10

Miller, J. Hillis, *56*

Minimum Foundations Program (public schools), 36–37

minorities: affirmative action and, 130; economic opportunity for, 109, 123. *See also* diversity; race

Missouri Plan (judicial merit system), 47

Mohl, Raymond, 124

Moore, Harry T., 37

mosquitoes, control of, 34

multiple-ballot law, 11

municipalities. *See* city government; city manager system; mayoral system

municipal service taxing units (MSTUs), use of, 108–9

Naples, urban sprawl in, 122

National Aeronautics and Space Administration (NASA), *99,* 104

National Association for the Advancement of Colored People (NAACP): bus boycotts and, *93;* Double V campaign of, 35; lynchings and, 18; murder of

state leader of, 37; state investigation of, 40

National Association of Broadcasters, *62*

National Guard (Florida), 23, 41

natural resources: constitutional protection of, 45–46; degradation of, 126–28; exploitation of, 14; legislation on, 67–68; urban sprawl's impact on, 75–76, 121. *See also* Everglades; real estate development; water management

New Deal, financial assistance in, 30–31, 34, 53, 110

Nixon, Richard M., 66, 67, *98*

North Broward Hospital District, 91

northeastern U.S., migrants from, 130

northern region: characteristics of, 3, 146–47; Democratic Party support in, 130; diminished power of, 40–42, 43–44; political dominance of, 32–33; racial developments and, 36–40; Republican Party support in, 70, 71; southeast coalition with, 72–73. *See also* southern culture

Ocala, southern culture of, 6

*Ocala Weekly Banner* (periodical), 20

Ocklawaha River. *See* Cross-Florida Barge Canal

Ocoee, blacks votes in, 18–19

Okaloosa County, Republican support in, 71

O'Malley, Tom, *134*

Orange County: local government in, 105–6; school districts in, 106; taxes in, 75

Orchard, population of, 104

Orlando: environmental degradation in, 126; influence of, 3; population of, 30, 120

Ormond Beach, political meeting at, 27

Overtown, 124

Pajcic, Steve, 69, 71

Palm Beach County: busing in, 123;

home-rule charter for, 106–7; local government in, 105; population of, 121

Panama City, laborers in, 33

pari-mutuel interests, 30

Pasco County, water supply in, 127

patronage: governor's use of, 86, 90–91; justices of the peace as, 102; nepotism in, 24; in special district boards, 106

Pearl City, minorities in, 122

Pensacola: local government in, 105; military in, 33–34

Pepper, Claude, 53, 56, 57, 58

Perot, Ross, 49

Perry, blacks attacked in, 19

phosphate industry, 15, 50

Pinellas County, water supply in, 127

plantation system, brought to Florida, 7

police: costs of, 125; KKK's link with, 60. See also state police

political parties: cabinet system and, 73, 86–87; coalitions between, 82, 83; constitutional amendment process and, 114; divisions between, 128, 132, 141, 144, 145; growth management and, 131–32; Speaker and President elections and, 81–83. See also Democratic Party; Republican Party

politics: central issues in, 13–16; changes in, 41–42, 43–44, 147–48; coalitions in, 72–73; complexity of, 5; conservatism in, 148–49; development of, 11–20; distinctiveness of, 4–5; folklore about, 118; fragmentation in, 32–33, 74–76; modernization and, 49–52, 65–66; one-party system in, 4; shortsightedness in, 118–19, 141, 149–50; "spoils system" of, 71; two-party system in, 4, 31; urban sprawl's impact on, 121; in World War II, 33–42. See also campaigns; elections; political parties

poll tax, 11–12

population: in 1900, xii, 1, 13; in 1920–30, 28; in 1940s, 35–36; in 1950, xiii; in 1960s and 1970s, 49–50; in 1990,

1–2; in 2000, 120; changes in, 31, 146–47; expansion of, 28, 30, 32–33, 119–20, 146; patterns of growth in, 2, 120–21. See also diversity

Populist movement, 11–12

Pork Chop Gang: legislature dominated by, xiii, 58, 79; reapportionment opposed by, 38; segregation supported by, 39

presidential elections: of 1928, 26; of 1956, 61; of 1976, 73; of 1996, 73; constitutional amendments on ballots in, 114; southern culture's influence on, 16. See also specific U.S. presidents

prisons, 75, 117. See also crime

Progressive movement, 13–16

Prohibition Party, 20, 24

property tax: development funded by, 143–44; homestead exemption in, 28, 125; limits on, 48, 125; schools funded by, 106; special districts funded by, 106

public: cynicism of, 68; government meetings open to, 4, 68; legislature distrusted by, 79–80

public officials: campaign costs for, 70; distrust of, 79–80, 149–50; filing fees for, 52, 70; fiscal disclosure required for, 46, 68; term limits for, 80, 85. See also governors; House of Representatives; legislators; Senate

public opinion: context for, 87–88; on governors as responsible, 87–88, 91; on taxes and services, 128–30; voting and, 128

public policy: boards' and commissions' role in, 88–89; citizen petitions' impact on, 49; growth management and, 130–32, 141, 145. See also social policy

race: Cuban Americans on, 51; growth management and, 145; as political issue, 12, 13, 16, 31–32, 44, 66, 74; reapportionment linked to, 38–40. See

race—*Cont'd*
  *also* African Americans; Jim Crow
  laws; race relations; racial caste system; segregation
race relations: constitutional reform
  and, 44; economic development and,
  38–42; postwar, 36–37; in World War
  I, 16–18; in World War II, 35–36. *See
  also* segregation
racial caste system: alliance movement
  and, 11–12; erosion of, 38–40; establishment of, 10–11; maintenance of,
  36–37, 41. *See also* segregation
railroad interests, 14, 15, 17, 23
Reagan, Ronald, 69–70
real estate development: control of, 107,
  141–44, 145; fraud in, 29; railroads
  and, 14; support for, 15–16; unregulated, 121–22
reapportionment: coalition for, 72–73;
  context for, 36, 38–40; effects of, 66–
  67; implementation of, 45, 74, 78;
  schedule for, 32, 80; U.S. Supreme
  Court decisions on, 41–42, 44–45
Reconstruction, process of, 9–11
regionalism: coalitions in, 72–73; divisions in, 6–7, 44, 76; statehood and,
  7. *See also* central region; northern
  region; southeastern region
religion, 8, 12. *See also* Catholic Church;
  Jewish Americans
Renick, Dick, *135*
Republican Party: on constitutional revision, 45; experience of, 70–71;
  growth management and, 132, 141;
  percentage registered as, 129–31; racial caste system resisted by, 10–11;
  renaissance of, 4, 31, 51–52, *61*, 69–
  74, 147–48; setbacks for, 65–66
resign to run law, 4
retirees. *See* senior citizens
Reubin O'D. Askew Institute on Politics
  and Society (University of Florida), xiii
Reubin O'D. Askew School of Public Administration and Policy (Florida State
  University), xiii
rights: in 1968 Constitution, 45–46;
  constitutional amendments related to,
  115; denied to African Americans, xii,
  10–12, 16, 18–19. *See also* voting
"right-to-work" provision, 45
Ritchie, Buzz, 82
roads: environmental degradation in
  construction of, 126; funds for, 126,
  128, 143, 144; modernization of, 35;
  racial motivation in development of,
  124; as social borders, 122
Robertson, Glenn W., 144
Rockefeller, John D., 15, 27
Rogers, Nell Foster, *64*
Roosevelt, Franklin Delano, 27, 30, 34.
  *See also* New Deal
Rosewood, blacks attacked in, 19
Rules Committee, 81, 83
rural areas: development in, 143; impact
  of poll tax on, 12; local government
  in, 104–5; population in, 13, 31; poverty in, 9, 13, 14; reapportionment
  and, 38–39

St. Augustine: civil rights campaign in,
  41, *94, 95;* politicians in, 22
St. Petersburg, population of, 28
sales tax: expansion of, 142–43; opposition to, 128–29; rate of, 125–26
saltwater, intrusion of, 126–27
Sansom, Dixie, *138*
Santa Rosa County, Republican support
  in, 71
schools: in African American neighborhoods, 122–24; censorship in, 40;
  costs of, 126; desegregation of, 39–41,
  *59, 60,* 123; funds for, 106, 116–17,
  129, *138,* 144; race relations and, 36–
  37; seizure of, 52, 65, *98;* as special
  districts, 106. *See also* busing
Seabreeze Beach (Daytona), automobiles on, *21*

secretary of state, role of, 87–88
segregation: abolishment of, 41–42; on beaches, *94*; codification of, xii, 9, 11; enforcement of, 11, 16; impact of urban sprawl on, 122–24; legal basis for undermined, 38–40; legislation in support of, 36–37; in political campaigns, *59*, *60*; resistance to, 18–19, 40–41; wartime mobilization and, 16–17, 35–36
Seminole Indians, *62*
Senate: budget responsibilities of, 84–85; powers of, 80–81; President of, 81–83, 84, 116, *138*; reapportionment and, 38–39; staff of, 83–84; term limits for, 80, 89–90; women in, *138*
senior citizens: health care for, 103; influence of, 50, 51, 147, 148; Republican Party support from, 70; settlement patterns of, 2–3, 120–21; social assistance for, 128
services: attitudes toward, 128–30, 145; county and city delivery of, 108–9; funds for, 124–28, 143; growth management and, 132; taxes on, 71, 143; for unincorporated areas, 107–8
Shevin, Robert, *134*
Sholtz, Gov. David, 27, 29–30
slavery, 8–9
Smathers, George, 51, *57*, *61*, *62*
Smith, Jim, 69, *137*
social class: as challenge to state elites, 12; growth management approach and, 132, 141; tax sentiments related to, 129
social policy: attitudes toward, 75, 128–30; federal and state roles in, 103; influences on, 50–51. *See also* Medicaid; services; welfare programs
social relations: changes in, 41–42, 43–44; development of, 11–20; impact of urban sprawl on, 121–24; problems in, 75–76; in World War II, 33–42
southeastern region: characteristics of, 3, 6; environmental concerns in, 67–68; hurricane in, *26*; northern coalition

with, 72–73; population in, 36, 120–21; water supply in, 126–27, 149
Southern Christian Leadership Conference (SCLC), 41, *94*, *95*
southern culture: economic development and, 38–39; influence of, 5, 11, 16; migration's impact on, 3–4, 7; presidential election and, 16; state's origins in, 6–7; undermined in development, 43–44, 76. *See also* Civil War
South Florida Water Management District, 105–6
space program, economic impact of, *99*, 104
special-interest groups, 80, 111
special-purpose districts: role of, 105–6; service provision and, 108–9
SSI (Supplemental Security Income), 110
Starke, Gov. Madison, 8
State Board of Education, 89
State Comprehensive Planning Act, 67–68
state government: constitutional revision and, 44–46, 115; distinctiveness of, 4; federal interaction with, 103–4; fragmentation of, 77–80, 83, 84, 85–87, 90, 102, 115–17, 148; growth management amd, 131–32, 141; modernization of, 49–52, 65–66, 74, 77–79, 119; openness in, 4, 68; power of, 102–3; reorganization of, 36, 46; structure of, 5, 147; transformation of, xii–xiv. *See also* executive branch; judiciary system; legislature
state police vs. civil rights protesters, 41
statute, definition of, 81
Stipanovich, J. M. "Mac," 124
Stone, Richard, 69, *134*
Sturkie resolution, 20
sugar industry: diminished influence of, 50; water pollution from, 126, 127–28
Supplemental Security Income (SSI), 110

Supreme Court (Fla.): African Americans on, *100*; appointments to, 47; neighborhood court experiment of, 102; role of, 91–92, 112
*Swann* v. *Adams*, 44–45

Tallahassee: bus boycott in, *93*; capital buildings in, *22*, 77, 115–16; local government in, 105; neighborhood court experiment in, 102; politics in, 73; schools in, *136*
Tampa: laborers in, 33; local government in, 105; population of, 28, 31, 120; urban sprawl of, 122
Taxation and Budget Reform Commission, 112
taxes: attitudes toward, 124–25, 128–30, 145, 148; committees and commissions on, 81, 88, 112; constitutional amendments related to, 115; in Great Depression, 29; growth management legislation and, 141–44; limits on, 48, 125, 148; petition on, 111; reform of, 68, 132, 141, 142; on services, 71, 143; structure of, 108–9, 125–26. *See also* budget; finances; income tax; property tax; sales tax; utility tax
Texas: Florida compared to, 49–50; immigration to, 103; population in, 120
timber industry: black workers and, 18; brought by migrants, 7; importance of, 31; support for, 15
Tin Can Tourist Camp (Gainesville), 25
Tippetts, Katherine, 19
tobacco industry, state suit against, 76, 91
tourism: crime and, 75; economic dominance of, 1, 25, 50; growth of, 40–41, 76; promotion of, 35, 41; revenues from, 75, 124, 125–26
Towey, Jim, 80–81
Trammell, Gov. Park, 18, 87
transportation: federal expenditures on, 34; funding of, 117. *See also* automobiles; railroad interests; roads

Transportation, Department of, 90
Turlington, Ralph, *137*
turpentine industry, 7, 18
two-party system, 4, 31

unincorporated areas, services for, 107–8
United States, population growth in, 120. *See also* presidential elections; *specific states*
U.S. Army Air Force, bases and training for, 34, 55
U.S. Census, reapportionment based on, 80
U.S. Congress: appointments and elections for, 90; continuity in, 79–80; legislation process in, 81
U.S. Constitution: amendments to, 19, 48, 102–3; state's rights in, 102–3
U.S. Navy, bases for, 33–34, 103–4
U.S. Office of Economic Opportunity, 109
U.S. Senate, 1980 primary for, 69
U.S. Supreme Court, on reapportionment, 41–42, 44–45. *See also specific cases*
universities, governance of, 90
University of Florida, xiii, 56
urban areas: cypress trees in, 126; delivery of services in, 108–9; growth of, 49–50, 107, 119–20; local government in, 104–5; problems of sprawl in, 119–24; water pollution from, 127–28. *See also* growth management
utility tax, schools funded by, 106

Veterans Affairs, Department of, 89. *See also* military
voter registration: by blacks, 37; party differences in, 66, 71–72, 129–31; by Republicans, 70, 71–72
voting: by African Americans, 18–19, 37, 41–42, 47–48, 51; blacks disfranchised in, xii, 11–12; conservatism in, 148–49; on constitutional amendments, 110–11, 114–15; constitutional

reform and, 47–48; by Cuban Americans, 51; poll tax on, 11–12; public opinion and, 128; by senior citizens, 50; by women, 19, 47–48
Voting Rights Act (1965), 41

Walt Disney World, 3, 41
Warren, Gov. Fuller, 35, 36, 37, *56*, *60*
water management: canal opposition and, 66–67, *96*; costs of, 125; environmental degradation and, 126–28, 149; special districts for, 90, 105–6
Water Resources Act, 67–68
Webster, Dan, 82
welfare programs: attitudes toward, 128–29; expansion of, 109–10; funds for, 143, 144
West Florida, statehood and, 7
Wetherell, T. K., 124–25

white primaries, outlawed, xiii, 38
white supremacy, 16, 19. *See also* Ku Klux Klan; racial caste system; segregation; southern culture
wildlife, degradation of, 127
women: political participation of, 43, 67, 69, *135*, *138*; rights demanded by, 19–20; voting by, 19, 47–48
Works Progress Administration, *53*
World War I: black migration during, 17–18; mobilization for, 16–17
World War II: economic growth and, xiii, 31–32, 33–36; Florida commissions during, 88; mobilization for, 32–33, *55*, 88, 103–4

Yulee, David Levy, 8

zoning, in growth management, 141–43